Science Projects About

Electricity and Magnets

Science Projects About
Electricity
and Magnets

Robert Gardner

•Science Projects •

ENSLOW PUBLISHERS, INC.

Bloy St. and Ramsey Ave.   P.O. Box 38
Box 777   Aldershot
Hillside, N.J. 07205   Hants GU12 6BP
U.S.A.   U.K.

Library of Congress Cataloging-in-Publication Data

Gardner, Robert, 1929-
　　Science projects about electricity and magnets / Robert Gardner.
　　　　p. cm. — (Science projects)
　　Includes bibliographical references and index.
　　ISBN 0-89490-530-9
　　　　1. Electricity—Experiments—Juvenile literature. 2. Magnets—
　　Experiments—Juvenile literature. 3. Science projects—Juvenile
　　literature. 4. Science—Exhibitions—Juvenile literature.
　　[1. Electricity—Experiments. 2. Magnets—Experiments.
　　3. Experiments. 4. Science projects.] I. Title. II. Series:
　　Gardner, Robert, 1929-　Science projects.
　　Q527.2.G384　1994
　　537'.078—dc20　　　　　　　　　　　　　　　　　93-45252
　　　　　　　　　　　　　　　　　　　　　　　　　　　　CIP
　　　　　　　　　　　　　　　　　　　　　　　　　　　　AC

Printed in the United States of America

10 9 8 7 6 5 4 3 2 1

Illustration Credits: Stephen F. Delisle

Cover Photo: © Stuart Simons, 1994

Contents

*appropriate for science fair project ideas.

8/22/94 Duncan

*appropriate for science fair project ideas.

Introduction

This book is filled with science projects and experiments about electricity and magnetism. Most of the materials you will need to carry out these activities can be found in your home or school. Several of the experiments may require materials that you can buy in a supermarket, a hobby shop, or a hardware store. You will need someone to help you with a few activities that require more than one pair of hands, and if any danger is involved, it will be indicated. It would be best if you work with friends or adults who enjoy experimenting as much as you do. In that way, you will both enjoy what you are doing.

Like a good scientist, you will find it useful to record your ideas, notes, data, and anything you can conclude from your experiments in a notebook. By so doing, you can keep track of the information you gather and the conclusions you reach. It will allow you to refer back to other experiments you have done that may be useful to you in projects you will do later.

Science Fairs

Some of the projects in this book may be appropriate for a science fair. Those projects are indicated with an asterisk (*). However, judges at such fairs do not reward projects or experiments that are simply copied from a book. For example, the use of flowing water serving as a model of electric current would probably not impress judges unless it was done in a novel or creative way. A more detailed model showing the source of the current, what happens to it, and an explanation of the limitations of water as a model for electricity would be likely to receive more consideration.

Science fair judges tend to reward creative thought and imagination. It is difficult to be creative or imaginative unless you are really interested in your project; consequently, it is wise to choose something that appeals to you. And before you jump into a project, consider, too, your own talents and the cost of materials you will need.

If you decide to use a project found in this book for a science fair, you should find ways to modify or extend the project. This should not be difficult because you will probably discover that as you do these projects new ideas for experiments will come to mind. These new experiments could make excellent science fair projects, particularly because the ideas are your own and are interesting to you.

If you decide to enter a science fair and have never done so before, you should read some of the books listed in the bibliography. The references that deal specifically with science fairs will provide plenty of helpful hints and lots of useful information that will enable you to avoid the pitfalls that sometimes plague first-time entrants. You will learn how to prepare appealing reports that include charts and graphs, how to set up and display your work, how to present your project, and how to relate to judges and visitors.

Safety First

Most of the projects included in this book are perfectly safe. However, the following safety rules are well worth reading before you start any project.

1. Do any experiments or projects, whether from this book or of your own design, under the supervision of a science teacher or other knowledgeable adult.

2. Read all instructions carefully before proceeding with a project. If you have questions, check with your supervisor before going any further.

3. Maintain a serious attitude while conducting experiments. Fooling around can be dangerous to you and to others.

4. Wear approved safety goggles when you are doing anything that might cause injury to your eyes.

5. Do not eat or drink while experimenting.

6. Have a first aid kit nearby while you are experimenting.

7. Do not put your fingers or any object other than properly designed electrical connectors into electrical outlets.

8. Never experiment with household electricity except under the supervision of a knowledgeable adult.

9. Do not touch a lit light bulb. Light bulbs produce light, but they also produce heat.

10. Never look directly at the sun. It can cause permanent damage to your eyes.

1

Electricity and Magnetism

Can you imagine what it would be like in a world without electric power? During the evening of November 11, 1965, millions of people found out. On that night, most of the northeastern United States was suddenly plunged into darkness. It was the largest power failure in history. People found themselves trapped in elevators, subways, and office buildings. Electrical machinery ground to a halt. Millions of homes were without not only lights but heat, refrigeration, stoves, and a variety of other comforts as well.

Since we depend on electricity for so many things in our lives, it is only reasonable that we have some understanding of the way it works. This book is designed to develop that understanding. The electricity used to run the lights and electrical appliances in your home or school is too dangerous for experiments. Consequently, in the experiments you will be doing, you will use such things as small magnets and wires, flashlight bulbs and batteries, nails, and other common, safe materials.

You may wonder how magnets are related to electricity. That is a good question. In fact, it was only about 175 years ago that the connection was accidentally discovered. You will see the connection in Chapter 4, but first you need to learn something about both magnets and electricity.

Magnetism

When he was four years old, Albert Einstein was given a toy magnetic compass by his father. At the age of 67, when he wrote his biography, Einstein recalled the joy and wonder he found in that simple toy. You too may have played with a magnetic compass and wondered why it always points in the same direction. Perhaps you placed a magnet near the compass and watched the compass needle swing wildly toward or away from the magnet.

In this chapter, we will experiment with magnets and examine the forces they exert. You may be surprised to find that materials not usually regarded as magnets may be affected by magnets. On the other hand, some materials are totally unaffected by magnets. Let's begin by seeing how two magnets affect each other.

1.1 *Two Magnets*

If you have bar magnets, one end is usually marked "N." The other end is marked "S." If you have small, flat, rubberized magnets, their sides are probably not marked, but you can place a small piece of tape on one face so that it can be identified (Figure 1-1). Take two identical magnets. Can you find two ends or two flat faces of the magnets that attract each other?

Things you'll need:

- two identical bar magnets or small, flat, square or rectangular magnets like the kind found in cabinet doors (Stores such as Radio Shack sell rubberized magnets such as these for very little cost.)
- thread
- tape

What happens if you separate the magnets and turn one magnet around? Do the magnets now attract or repel each other? What happens if you turn both magnets around? Do they attract or repel each other now?

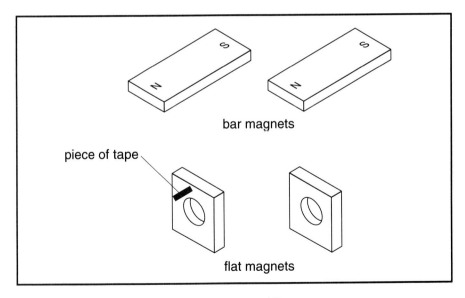

Figure 1-1) Bar magnets and flat magnets.

Hang one of the magnets from a long thread so it is free to turn. You can tape the free end of the thread to a door frame, the side of a table or chair, or a cabinet—just be sure that the magnet is free to turn at the end of the long thread and that it is far from any big metallic objects.

Now test your powers of prediction. How can you use the second magnet to attract the magnet that is suspended from a thread? Predict a way it can be done. Then test your prediction. Were you right?

Since you know how to attract the suspended magnet, predict what you need to do to repel the suspended magnet with the second magnet. Then test your prediction. Were you right?

Magnetic Poles

If you have a bar magnet, it may have an "N" on one end and an "S" on the other. The "N" stands for north and the "S" for south. These are called the poles of the magnet. Every magnet has a north pole and a south pole. Flat magnets have a north pole on one face and a south pole on the opposite face. To see why the poles are called north and south, you can do the next experiment.

1.2 Identifying a Magnet's Poles*

Hang a bar magnet or a flat magnet from a long thread as shown in Figure 1-2. If you use a magnet that has its poles marked "N" and "S," cover the letters with a small piece of masking tape as shown in Figure 1-2. You can attach the free end of the thread to a ceiling or a door

Things you'll need:

- two bar magnets or flat magnets
- thumbtack or tape
- masking tape
- thread
- magnetic compass

frame with a thumbtack or tape. Be sure the magnet is free to swing and is far from any other metallic objects.

Wait until the magnet stops moving. You will see that it is aligned in a particular direction. Turn the magnet slightly. Does it stay where you turned it, or does it return to its original position?

You will find that one end or face of the magnet is turned toward the north. That is why people call that end of the magnet the north pole or, better, the north-seeking pole. A small magnet that is free to turn inside a closed container is called a magnetic compass. Compasses are used to navigate ships and airplanes. They were probably first used by Chinese explorers nearly 2,000 years ago and have been used by European sailing vessels since the eleventh century.

Now that you have identified the north-seeking pole of the suspended magnet, you know that the pole at the other end or side of the magnet is the south-seeking pole. Label the proper ends of your magnet "N" for north and "S" for south. Repeat the experiment with a second magnet and label its poles too.

You now have two magnets, and you have identified the poles of each one. What will happen if you bring the north-seeking pole of one magnet close to the north-seeking pole of a second magnet? Do the poles attract or repel one another? What happens to a north-seeking pole and a south-seeking pole? Do they attract or repel? Do like poles (north-seeking and north-seeking or south-seeking and south-seeking) attract or repel one another? What about unlike magnetic poles?

Hold a magnetic compass far from any metallic objects. You will see that one end of the compass needle, like any magnet, points northward. Which pole of the magnetic compass is this? Now slowly move the north-seeking pole of a magnet toward the north-seeking pole of the compass needle. (Do not get too close or you may reverse the polarity of the magnetic compass.) What happens? What happens when you slowly move the south-seeking pole of a magnet toward the north-seeking pole of the compass needle?

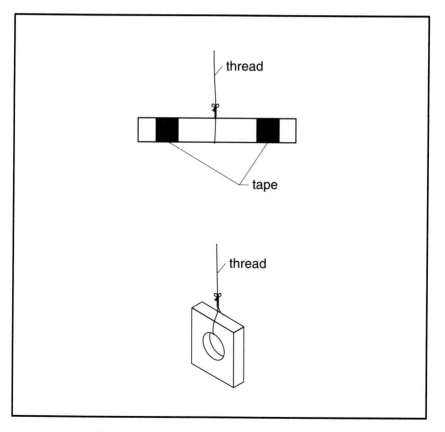

Figure 1-2a) A suspended bar magnet b) flat magnet.

Exploring on Your Own

- You can make a magnetic compass of your own. Begin by stroking a sewing needle with a strong magnet as shown in Figure 1-3. Be sure to always stroke the magnet in the same direction as shown in the drawing. After about a dozen strokes, grip one end of the needle. Bring the other end of the needle near a magnetic compass. Which end of the needle is the north-seeking pole? Does it also have a south-seeking pole?

- Place the magnetized needle on a thin piece of cork, or have an adult help you drip a glob of candle wax around the center of the needle. The idea is to use the cork to make the needle float in a container of water. Can you use the needle to determine which direction is north? (If the needle keeps moving to the edge of the container, add a drop of soapy water to the container.)

- You can make another kind of magnetic compass by hanging a magnetized needle from a thread in a covered glass or clear plastic jar. Can you use this compass to determine direction?

- Can you change a nail into a magnet? To find out, stroke a nail as you did the needle in Figure 1-3, then move one end of the nail toward a magnetic compass. How does it affect the compass needle? What happens if you turn the nail around? Have you succeeded in making the nail into a magnet?

- Fill a small test tube with iron filings. Put a stopper in the tube and stroke it with a magnet as you did the needle and nail. Then bring the tube near a magnetic compass. Have you made the iron filings into a magnet? Now shake the tube and again bring it near the compass. What happens?

- Will a solid magnet also lose its magnetism if it is shaken? To find out, shake a needle or nail that you have made into a magnet. Then hold it near a magnetic compass. Has it lost its magnetism? Will it lose its magnetism if you drop it many times?

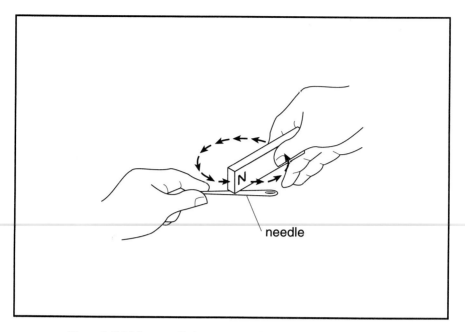

needle

Figure 1-3) Make a needle into a magnet by stroking it with a magnet.

- How are magnetic forces similar to the force of gravity? How are these two forces different?

Just for Fun

- Use a magnet under a table to move a steel ball or a small toy steel car along a table top. If you have several magnets, you and your friends can race cars or other objects along a magnetically powered race track.

- Make a small toy boat from a piece of scrap wood. Tape a steel screw to the bottom of the boat, and place the boat in a large water-filled plastic container. With a magnet, you can steer your boat around the plastic-enclosed "lake."

- Make a list of all the places where magnets are used in your home or school.

The Magnetic Earth

Since we can use a magnetic compass to determine directions on the earth, the earth itself must be like a giant magnet. In fact, we can think of the earth as if it had a giant magnet buried within it as shown in Figure 1-4. The pole of this "giant magnet" that is located near the northern end of the planet is a south-seeking pole. Remember, the north-seeking pole of a magnet is attracted to a south-seeking pole and repelled by another north-seeking pole. Since the north-seeking poles of magnets are attracted northward, the pole at the northern end of the earth must be a south-seeking pole.

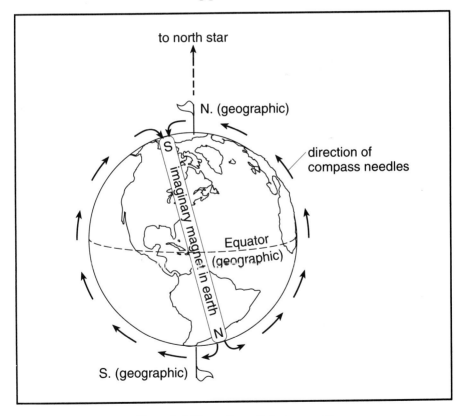

Figure 1-4) The earth as a "giant magnet."

The earth's magnetic poles are not located at the same places as its geographic north and south poles. Furthermore, the earth's magnetism is affected by the composition of the earth, which varies from place to place. As a result, the direction that a north-seeking compass needle points varies with location as shown in Figure 1-5. Around Boston, a compass needle actually points about fifteen degrees west of true north (the direction that points toward the North Pole). Near San Diego, the compass points about fifteen degrees east of true north. In Florida, compass needles point almost toward the geographic North Pole. Only along a line called the agonic line does a magnetic compass point toward true north.

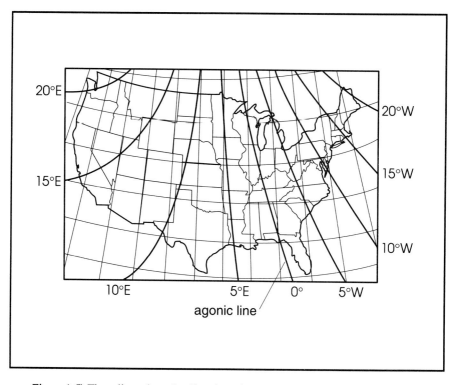

Figure 1-5) These lines show the directions that a compass needle points relative to true north.

The Earth's Reversing Magnetism

Geologists have found that the earth's magnetism has been reversed several times. That is, the earth's magnetic poles have been switched during its long history. Recent drillings taken from the ocean bottom contained magnetic grains that indicated that the earth's magnetic poles were reversed for a period of 10,000 years as recently as 1.1 million years ago.

1.3 Magnetic and Nonmagnetic Matter*

As you probably know, not everything acts like a magnet. Some things are not even attracted by a magnet. In this experiment, you will test a number of items to see how they behave with respect to magnets.

Use file cards and tape to make three cards that enclose a magnet, an iron washer, and a square piece of cardboard: Fold each card in half. Unfold the cards, and on each one, tape one object. Fold the cards to cover the objects, and seal the edges with tape. (See Figure 1-6.) Then ask a friend to test each of the three cards by bringing them, one at a time, near the north-seeking and then the south-seeking pole of a magnet. Can he or she determine which card contains a magnet? Can you identify the objects in a similar set of cards that your friend has prepared for you?

Why is it so easy to identify the card that encloses the cardboard? What is different about the way the iron washer and the magnet behave in the presence of another magnet?

Now test a variety of objects with a magnet. You might use another magnet, coins, paper, nails, copper wire, iron wire, plastic, chalk, etc. Divide the objects into three groups: (1) things that are attracted and repelled by opposite poles of a magnet; (2) things that are attracted by both poles of a magnet; (3) things that are not affected by either pole of a magnet.

What kinds of objects do you find in each group? Are all metals attracted to magnets? If an object is attracted to a magnet, does that mean the object is itself a magnet?

Things you'll need:

- file cards
- masking tape
- iron washers
- small, flat magnets
- assorted materials—paper, plastic, cardboard, copper, chalk, cloth, wood, aluminum, coins, etc.

Exploring on Your Own

- Use a compass and a straight stick or pencil to make a "sundial compass" clock. Hold the compass in sunlight. Turn the compass so that the "N" on its dial lies beneath the north-seeking end of the compass needle. Orient the stick or pencil vertically over the "S" on the dial. Notice that the shadow of the pencil or stick falls on the face of the compass. How can you use your sundial compass to tell the approximate time? Using the information in Figure 1-5, figure out a way to make your "clock" more accurate.

- You can easily lift a paper clip with a magnet. But will the magnetism act through paper? To find out, place a small piece of paper over the paper clip. Will the magnet attract the paper clip through the

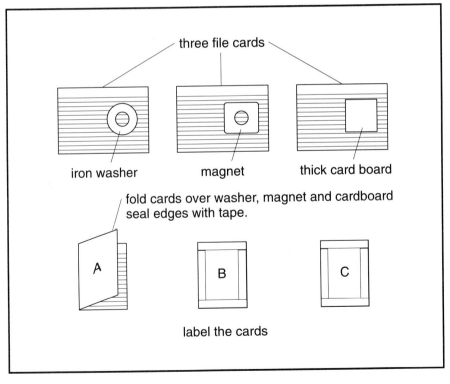

Figure 1-6) Preparing mystery cards.

paper? Will the magnet act through cardboard? Through plastic? Through water? Wood? Copper? How about iron?

- With a strong magnet, you can make a paper clip "float" in air at the end of a piece of thread as shown in Figure 1-7. What do you predict will happen if you slide a piece of paper between the paper clip and the magnet? What about a thin piece of plastic? A thin piece of wood or cardboard? The lid from a metal can?

- How does the distance between the pole of a magnet and an object it attracts affect the force that the magnet exerts on the object? One way to find out is to lift a metal can lid with a magnet. Then see how many pieces of cardboard or paper you can place between the magnet and the lid and still lift the lid.

Just for Fun

- Drop a paper clip into a cup of water. Challenge friends or members of your family to remove the paper clip without spilling the water or placing anything in the water. After they give up, you can use a magnet to pull the paper clip along the sides of the container to the top.

- Tell your friends that you will "cut" the invisible lines of force that attract the paper clip to the magnet in the setup shown in Figure 1-7. Then use a pair of scissors to "cut" the space between the paper clip and the magnet. The paper clip will fall when you "cut" the space between the magnet and the paper clip just as you predicted. (Remember what happened when the can lid was placed between the magnet and the paper clip.)

- Mix some iron filings with some salt or sugar. Then use a magnet to separate the black iron filings from the white crystals.

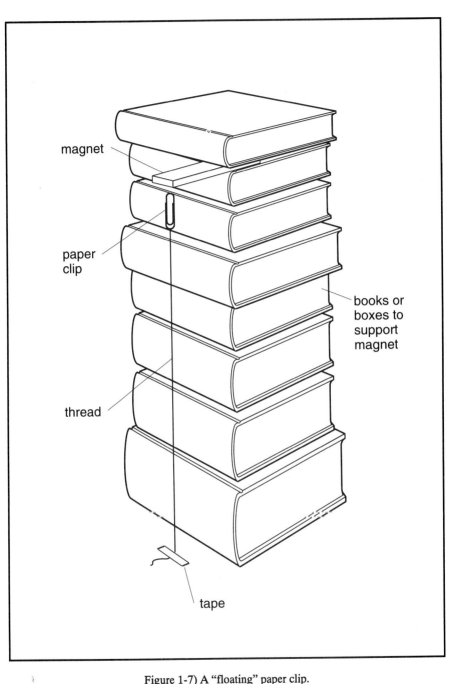

magnet

paper
clip

books or
boxes to
support
magnet

thread

tape

Figure 1-7) A "floating" paper clip.

25

1.4 Magnetic Patterns

Michael Faraday was a brilliant, self-educated scientist who lived in the 1800's. His interest, hard work, and enthusiasm led him to discover a great many things about electricity and magnetism. In one of his experiments, he sprinkled some iron filings on a thin sheet of cardboard that he had placed over a bar magnet. You can do the same experiment he did.

Things you'll need:

- bar magnet
- iron filings (or small pieces of steel wool)
- magnetic compass(es)
- piece of cardboard
- white paper
- scissors

Place a bar magnet on a nonmetallic table or floor. Tape a sheet of white paper onto a piece of cardboard. Then place the cardboard (white-paper-side up) on top of the magnet. Sprinkle some iron filings onto the paper and gently tap the cardboard. Describe the pattern that you see.

If you do not have iron filings, use scissors to cut some steel wool into very short lengths of fine wire. Then sprinkle these tiny bits of steel wool onto the paper and tap the cardboard. You will obtain the same type of pattern.

To Faraday, who was a very visual thinker, the pattern formed by the tiny bits of iron revealed what he called lines of magnetic force. Together these lines of force constitute what we call the magnetic field around the magnet. The field is always present around the magnet. The pattern of the magnetic lines of force is made visible by the tiny bits of iron we sprinkle around the magnet. These bits of iron "feel" the effect of the magnetic forces and line up in the direction of the force at each position. Faraday pointed out that the magnetic forces are greatest where the lines of force are closest together.

The pattern of the magnetic field around a bar magnet can also be mapped with one or more magnetic compasses. Place the compass or compasses at various places around the magnet. Mark on the paper a little arrow head at the location of the north-seeking pole of the compass needle. Put a dash at the south-seeking end of the needle. After you have done this many times, you will see the pattern of magnetic lines of force around the magnet.

The drawing in Figure 1-8 shows the pattern made when many compasses are placed around a bar magnet. Is the pattern similar to the one that you made by drawing the direction of the compass needle at many locations?

Exploring on Your Own

- To get a three-dimensional view of a magnetic field, put about a tablespoonful of short pieces of steel wool in a full, transparent, plastic bottle of baby oil. There should be no air in the bottle when the cap is screwed back on. To be sure there is no air in the bottle, squeeze the bottle gently until a little oil spills over its rim. Then maintain your squeeze as you screw the cap back on the bottle.

Now you can view lines of magnetic force in 3-D. Place the bottle between the poles of two magnets. What does the pattern between two like magnetic poles look like? (Of course, you will need two magnets to find out.) What does the pattern between two unlike poles look like? What about the pattern between the two poles of a horseshoe magnet?

Electricity

You have probably had experience with electricity even though you may not have been aware of it. In the winter, you may have gotten an electric shock when you reached for a metal door handle after walking across a rug or sliding across the plastic seatcovers in a car. In a dark room, you have probably seen the sparks produced by moving electric charges when you pulled a sweater over your head. Lightning is made in a similar way but on a much larger scale.

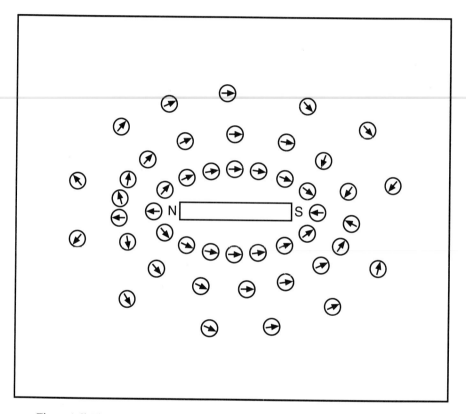

Figure 1-8) The pattern of magnetic lines of force around a bar magnet as mapped by many magentic compasses.

It is possible to do experiments with electricity that are very similar to the ones you have done with magnets. However, these experiments require dry air, that is, very low humidity. On a humid day, these experiments are impossible to do because electric charges leak away in damp air. Consequently, both the experiments and their results will be described. In the winter when it is cold outside, chances are the air inside you home or school will be quite dry. In that case, you can do these experiments for yourself and confirm the results. If weather conditions are not good, you will find the experiments very frustrating. The experiments described here were done in very dry air.

Electrical Attraction and Repulsion

The experimenters made a sling from a piece of plastic-covered wire like the one shown in Figure 1-9 and suspended it by a long thread. They rubbed a plastic (polyethylene) ruler with a woolen cloth and placed it in the sling. When a second identical ruler was rubbed with wool and held near the first one, the ruler in the sling swung away from the other one. It was clear that the two rulers repelled one another. You might think the rulers had been turned into magnets, but a magnetic compass needle in a metal case was not affected by either ruler. You could say that the rulers had been charged by rubbing them with wool. Since both rulers had been charged in the same way, you can see that like charges repel each other as do the like poles of two magnets.

The experimenters then rubbed a number of other objects. A glass tube that had been rubbed with silk attracted the plastic ruler. The glass tube was then placed in the sling. When another glass tube was rubbed with silk and placed near the one in the sling, the two tubes repelled one another. But both tubes were attracted to a plastic ruler that had been rubbed with wool.

All the other objects that were charged in this way either attracted or repelled the plastic ruler. However, any object that attracted the charged plastic ruler would repel the charged glass test tube. This was true of all the things that could be charged. (The experimenters found they could not charge metallic objects that were held in their hands.) These results suggest there are only two kinds of charge.

Benjamin Franklin had done similar experiments more than 200 years ago. He defined the charge acquired by a glass tube rubbed with silk to be positive. When a test tube was rubbed with silk and held near a tube that had been rubbed with wool, the tubes repelled each other. According to Franklin, therefore, the glass tube rubbed with wool also carried a positive charge. Consequently, the plastic ruler in the experiments described must have the other kind of charge.

Franklin had defined the charge carried by a hard rubber rod rubbed with cat's fur to be negative. A rubber rod that had been rubbed with cat's fur was held near a plastic ruler that had been rubbed with wool. As you might guess, the ruler was repelled by the rubber rod. Both were negatively charged.

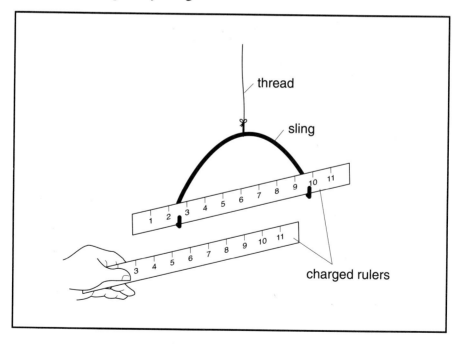

Figure 1-9) Like charges repel.

Since the plastic became negatively charged when rubbed with wool, you might expect the wool to become positively charged during the rubbing. To test this idea, the wool used to charge the plastic ruler was held near the ruler as it rested in a sling. The ruler swung toward the wool. The two objects carried opposite charges. This can be easily explained. As negative charges were transferred from the wool to the ruler, the woolen cloth was left with an excess of positive charges.

From all this, you can conclude that two kinds of electric charge are associated with matter—positive and negative—names that we took from Franklin's original experiment.

Measuring Charge

An electroscope is used to detect and determine the sign (+ or -) of electric charge. You can probably find one in your school's science laboratory. An electroscope like the one shown in Figure 1-10a can be charged by touching the metal knob with a charged object such as a plastic ruler that has been rubbed with wool. The greater the charge transferred to the electroscope, the greater the deflection of the metal leaf inside the electroscope.

The electroscope can also be charged by induction. That is, electric charge can be made to flow on or off the electroscope without physical contact with a charged object, as shown in Figure 1-10b. Drawing 1 in Figure 1-10b shows a finger touching the knob of an electroscope. In drawing 2, a charged object is brought near the electroscope. Like charge is repelled as far away as possible. In this case, negative charges are repelled to the body of the person touching the electroscope. The finger is then removed from the electroscope *before* the charged object is taken away. Since negative charges were driven from the electro-scope, an excess of positive charge remains. This excess positive charge is attracted to the negatively charged object near the knob at the top of the electroscope (drawing 3). Finally, the charged object is removed, and positive charges, which repel each other, spread over

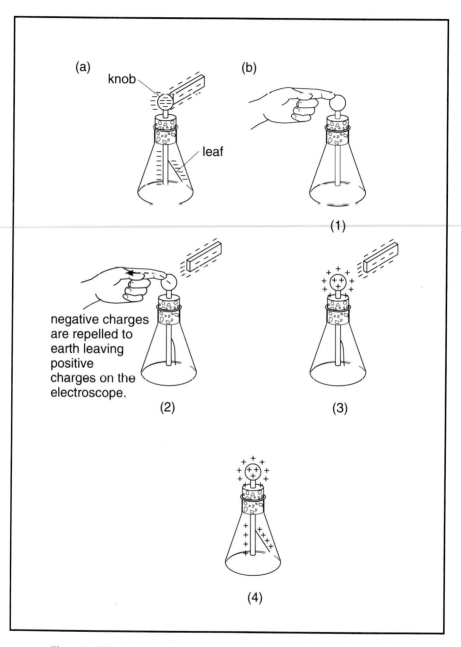

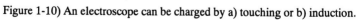

the electroscope. The positive charges on the leaf and the rest of the electroscope repel each other and so the leaf swings outward (drawing 4).

If a negatively charged object is now brought near the top of the electroscope, the leaf will fall because positive charges will be attracted toward the top of the electroscope. However, if a positively charged object is held near the knob, the leaf will swing farther outward. The leaf is repelled even more by the additional positive charges pushed down from the knob of the electroscope.

As you can see, an electroscope with a known charge can be used to detect the sign (+ or -) of a charged object. The amount of charge on the electroscope can be estimated by the amount that the leaf swings outward.

Exploring on Your Own

- Suspend a piece of puffed breakfast cereal from a long thread. If you bring a glass test tube near the piece of cereal, nothing should happen because neither object carries an electric charge. Now rub the test tube with cloth, paper, or plastic wrap and slowly bring it near the puffed cereal. You will see that it attracts the cereal. But how can this be? The cereal is not charged.

  Remember what you learned about induced charge. Charges in the piece of cereal will be attracted or repelled by the charged test tube as it is brought close to the cereal. Positive charges will move as far from the positively charged test tube as possible. Negative charges will move as close as possible. Because the negative charges in the puff of cereal are now closer to the glass tube than are the negative charges, the attractive force will be stronger than the repelling force. The puffed cereal moves toward the charged test tube. Why is the puffed cereal repelled when it touches the test tube?

  Rub a phonograph record with a cloth. Will the record attract the piece of puffed cereal?

- Suspend two balloons from the ends of two long pieces of thread. The balloons should be side by side and just a couple of inches apart. Charge both balloons with a piece of wool or fur. Do the balloons attract or repel? Now rub a third balloon with a piece of plastic wrap or a plastic sandwich bag. What happens when you bring this balloon near either of the other two?

- We *see* lightning and *hear* the thunder created by the lightning. Light travels at a speed of 300,000 km/s (186,000 mi/s); the speed of sound through air is about 340 m/s (0.21 mi/s). Because light travels so fast, we see lightning at almost the instant it happens. However, if the lightning is a mile away, it will take about five seconds before we hear the thunder that accompanies the lightning. (If it is a kilometer away, it will take about three seconds.) If you see lightning and then measure the time before you hear thunder, how can you tell how far away the storm is? **Lightning is very dangerous! If the storm is close by, get inside a house or a car. By all means do not stand outside under a tall object such as a tree.** Lightning occurs when charges in the clouds attract opposite charges from the earth. These charges move to the top of trees and other tall objects. The attraction between the charges in the clouds and the tall objects is what causes a larger charge—a bolt of lightning—to "jump" between the two objects.

Just for Fun

- Allow a very thin stream of water to flow from a faucet into a sink. Rub a plastic comb or ruler vigorously with a piece of cloth. Bring the charged comb or ruler close to the narrow stream of water. You will see the stream bend toward the charged object. (This will only work on a dry day. For best results, try it in a warm room on a bright, cold winter's day.) Use the same charged comb or ruler to pick up tiny pieces of paper, to attract grains of salt or gelatin, or to pull on floating soap bubbles.

- On a dry day, rub a balloon on your clothing or your hair. Hold the balloon close to your ear. Listen carefully! You will hear charges jump from the balloon to your ear. Then hold the balloon against a wall or ceiling. You will find the balloon "sticks" to the wall. Charges induced in the wall by the charged balloon result in an attracting electrical force.

- Take a piece of paper about three inches by five inches and cut it into eight lengthwise strips, leaving a narrow, uncut border along one of the three-inch sides of the paper. Hold the paper against a wall and rub it with a plastic bag or plastic wrap. When you lift the paper from the wall, the paper strips will repel one another, and you will have an eight-legged spider!

- Rub panty hose with a stretchable (polyethylene) plastic bag. You will see the panty hose fill out as the like charges repel one another.

Magnets and Electricity

You have seen that magnets always have a south-seeking pole and a north-seeking pole. You have seen too that the like poles of two magnets (north and north or south and south) repel each other and the opposite poles (north and south) attract. In the case of electricity, there appear to be two kinds of charge, positive (+) and negative (-). Like charges (+ and + or - and -) repel, and unlike charges (+ and -) attract. Early scientists suspected, as you might, that this similarity in behavior meant that magnetism and electricity were somehow related. But for centuries, no one could see how. Though both magnetic poles and electric charges appeared to obey the same laws of attraction and repulsion, the connection between them remained a mystery.

2

Batteries, Bulbs, and Wires

You turn a switch in a dark room. Suddenly the room is filled with light! It all seems so easy, but what makes the light go on? In the investigations that follow, you will learn what makes a light bulb light, how light bulbs can be connected together, and some of the reasons why they may not work. You will begin with basic materials—a battery, a bulb, and a wire.

Batteries wear out with use. Consequently, in all the experiments you will be doing with batteries and bulbs, do not light the bulbs longer than is needed to make your observations.

2.1 Light a Bulb

Using the three items shown in Figure 2-1, see if you can make the bulb light. In how many different ways can you make the bulb light? List them. Make another list of all the ways that do not work. Better

Things you'll need:
- flashlight bulb
- 6-in. (15 cm) length of bare copper wire
- D-cell (flashlight battery)

still, make drawings of what works and what does not work.

From your experiment, can you figure out what must be done to make a bulb light? Write a rule that explains how to make a bulb light.

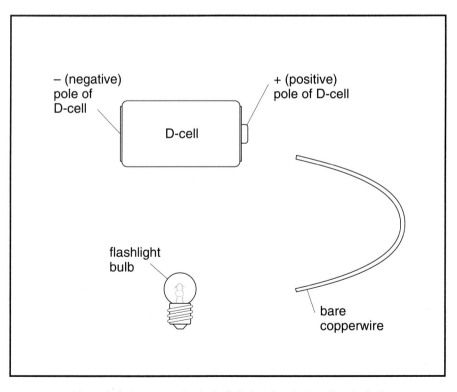

Figure 2-1) Can you make the bulb light using the D-cell and wire?

2.2 A Second Wire

In this experiment, you will find it helpful to work with another person because you will be using two wires. Make the bulb light as you did before. Once the bulb is glowing, have your partner use the

Things you'll need:
- flashlight bulb
- two 6-in. (15 cm) lengths of bare copper wire
- D-cell (flashlight battery)

second wire to connect the two terminals of the battery (positive and negative) as shown in Figure 2-2. What happens to the bulb when the battery terminals are connected by the second wire? **Do not connect the second wire for more than a few seconds. If left connected, it can wear out the battery quickly.**

What happens to the bulb when the second wire is removed?

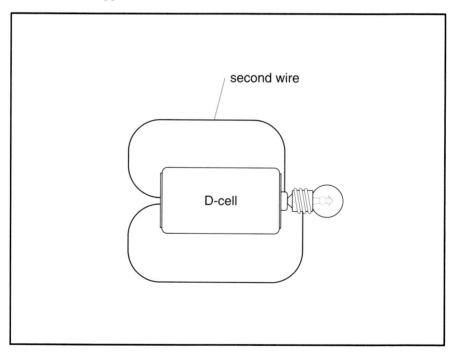

Figure 2-2) A second wire connects the + and - ends of the D-cell.

Circuits and Short Circuits

When one terminal of a battery is connected to the other by a light bulb and wire, an electric circuit is formed. Connections between other electrical devices and the terminals of a battery or between a building's electrical system and the local power company are electric circuits too. The light bulbs, toasters, radios, television sets, and other electrical devices in your home are parts of electric circuits. These circuits are connected to the wires that enter your home from the power company. **Never touch or play with the electric circuits found in your home or other buildings. They can be very dangerous!**

If the terminals of a battery are directly connected by a wire, a short circuit is formed. As you saw in Experiment 2.2, adding a short circuit will turn off the bulb in a regular electric circuit. Short circuits that occur in household circuits can cause fires. To disconnect these dangerous short circuits, most household circuits contain fuses that burn out, or circuit breakers that open, when short circuits occur, turning off the electricity in that circuit.

Inside a Bulb

If possible, find an adult who will take apart a flashlight bulb or a regular household bulb for you. **Do not attempt to do this by yourself—you might get cut.** Or your might look inside a large, clear, household bulb. You will find that the connections inside the bulb look like those shown in Figure 2-3. Notice how the metal parts at the bottom and the side of the bulb are connected to the bulb's filament— the thin wire in the middle of the bulb that glows when it is turned on. Do you see now why the bulb lights only when the opposite terminals of the battery are connected to special places on the bulb?

Exploring on Your Own

- Before you make the connections for each of the arrangements shown in Figure 2-4, see if you can predict whether or not the bulb will light. Why do you think the bulb will or will not light? Were all your predictions correct? If not, can you now explain why the bulb does or does not light in those cases where your predictions were not right?

- Take a flashlight apart. See if you can figure out how it works.

Just for Fun

- Build a flashlight of your own.

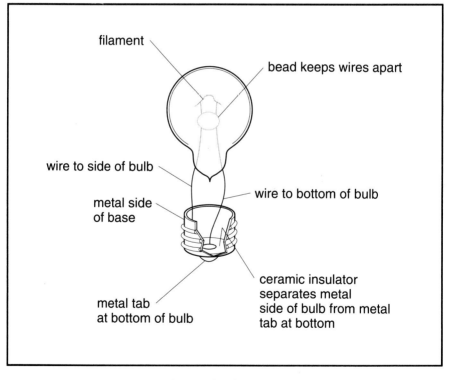

Figure 2-3) Inside a bulb.

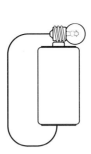

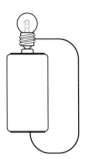
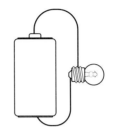

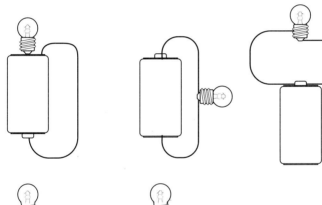

Figure 2-4) In which arrangements will the bulb light? In which arrangements will it not light?

2.3 Bulb and Battery Holders

You have found several ways to make a bulb light using a flashlight battery (D-cell) and a wire. Of course, you can connect more than one bulb to a battery and more than one battery to a bulb. However, it is difficult to make all these connections when you have to hold the bulbs, wires, and batteries with your hands. In this experiment, you will make some battery holders and some bulb holders. This will allow you to build more complicated circuits. If you already have battery holders and bulb sockets, like the ones shown in Figures 2-5a and 2-6a you can skip this experiment.

You can make a bulb holder with a clothespin taped to a piece

Things You'll Need:
- flashlight bulbs
- 4 D-cells (flashlight batteries)
- piece of soft wood
- spring-type clothespins
- wire
- strong, wide rubber bands
- paper clips
- tape
- thumbtacks
- Fahnestock clips (spring binding posts can be obtained from a science supply house or hardware store)
- mailing tube
- 5 metal tabs

of soft wood as shown in Figure 2-5b. Be sure the jaws of the clothespin are directly over the thumbtack. The jaws of the clothespin hold a wire firmly against the metal sides of the bulb. The tape holds the clothespin in place and forces the metal contact at the bottom of the bulb against a thumbtack that holds the second wire in place.

A variety of homemade battery holders are shown in Figure 2-6. In Figure 2-6b, a strong, wide rubber band is used to hold Fahnestock clips against the terminals (poles) of a battery. Connecting wires may be attached to the Fahnestock clips.

In Figure 2-6c, tape is used to hold paper clips firmly against each end of the battery. Connecting wires should probably have alligator clips at their ends to clamp onto the paper clips. However, you can use clothespins to hold wires in place if you do not have alligator clips. You might also use paper clips or paper fasteners. The wires used to connect bulbs and other devices to the battery shown in Figure 2-6d should have alligator clips. This battery is very useful because it is so easy to connect a circuit to one, two, three, or four D-cells.

Batteries are made up of electric cells. Technically, a D-cell, which is often referred to as a flashlight battery, is not a battery. It is a single electric cell. A true battery consists of two or more electric cells connected positive to negative as in Fig. 2-6d. We say these cells are connected *in series*. The battery shown in Fig. 2-6d consists of a mailing tube into which you can slide four D-cells together so that the

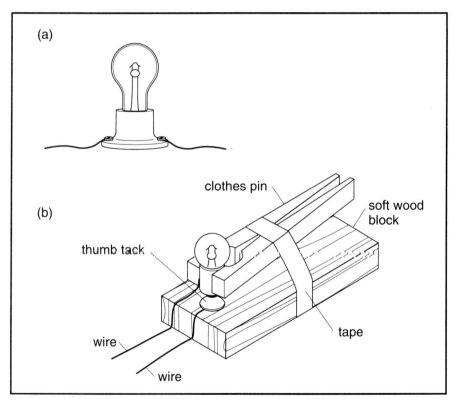

Figure 2-5) Bulb holders.

positive pole of one cell touches the negative pole of the next. If you make this battery, **have an adult cut a slot lengthwise along the top of the tube.** This will allow you to slide metal tabs between the terminals of the cells aligned in series as well as at each end of the battery.

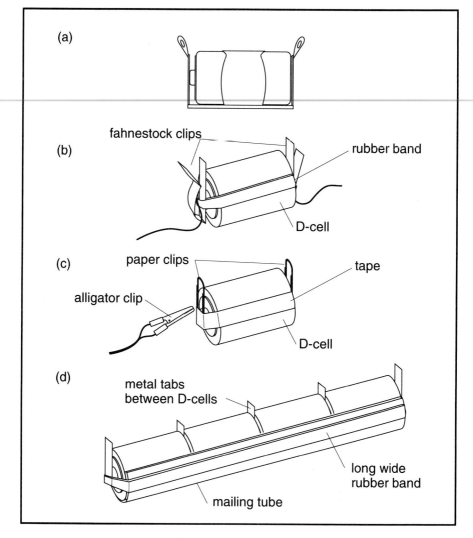

Figure 2-6) Battery holders.

2.4 Series and Parallel Circuits*

Now that you can hold bulbs and batteries without using your hands, you can build circuits with more than one bulb and D-cell. When people who work with electricity build a circuit, they do not draw detailed pictures of each of the parts. Instead, they use symbols. The symbols used to represent

Things you'll need:
- 2 flashlight bulbs
- 2 battery holders
- 2 D-cells (flashlight batteries)
- 4 wires (preferably with alligator clips)
- 2 bulb holders

electric cells, bulbs, and wires are shown in Figure 2-7.

In Figure 2-8, you see drawings of batteries, wires, and bulbs in a variety of circuits. Beside each circuit is a diagram of the same circuit using the symbols for batteries, bulbs, and wires.

Look at the circuits shown in Figure 2-8. As you can see, you have already built the circuit shown in 2-8a. Set up this simple circuit again so you can see how bright a single bulb shines when connected to a single D-cell.

In all the circuits shown in Figure 2-8, the bulbs are meant to be identical and so are the D-cells. In building the following circuits, be sure to use identical bulbs and cells.

Now build the circuit shown in Figure 2-8b, which has two D-cells connected in series. How does the brightness of the bulb in this circuit compare with that of the bulb connected to a single D-cell? What do you think will happen if you remove one of the D-cells from its holder? Try it! Were you right? Replace the D-cell so that the light comes on again. What will happen if you remove the other D-cell from its holder?

Build the circuit shown in Figure 2-8c. It has two D-cells side by side. Their positive terminals are connected and so are their negative terminals. Batteries (or bulbs) wired in this way are said to be wired *in parallel.* This is logical because the cells are side by side like parallel lines. If you think about it, it is the same as having a D-cell that is twice as big as an ordinary D-cell. How does the brightness of the bulb in this circuit compare with the brightness of the bulb in Figure 2-8a? Do you think the bulb will still light if you remove one of the D cells from its holder? Were you right?

In Figure 2-8d, the bulbs are in series and connected to a single D-cell. How does the brightness of each bulb compare with the brightness of the bulb in Figure 2-8a? Try to explain your observation. Remove one of the bulbs from its holder. Why does the other bulb go out? Now replace the bulb so that both bulbs light. What do you think will happen if you remove the other bulb from its holder? Were you right?

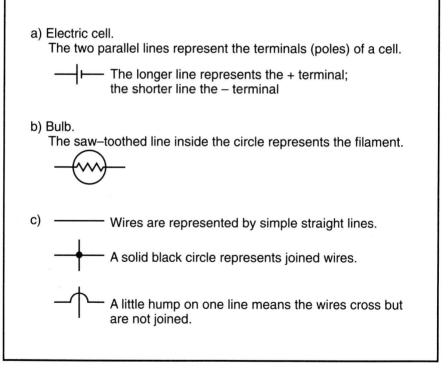

a) Electric cell.
   The two parallel lines represent the terminals (poles) of a cell.

   The longer line represents the + terminal;
   the shorter line the − terminal

b) Bulb.
   The saw–toothed line inside the circle represents the filament.

c) ──── Wires are represented by simple straight lines.

   A solid black circle represents joined wires.

   A little hump on one line means the wires cross but are not joined.

Figure 2-7) Electric symbols.

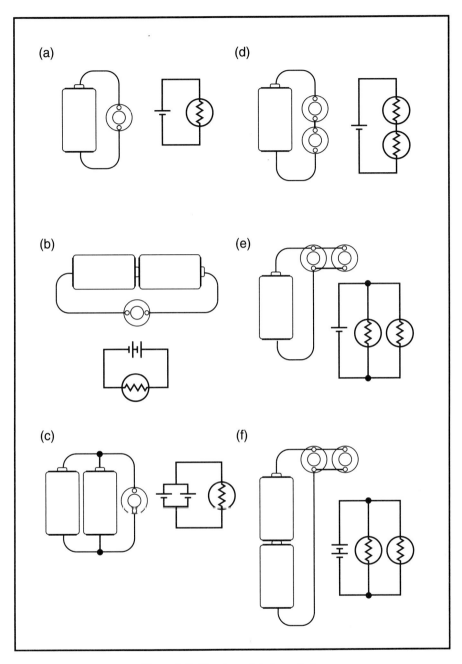

Figure 2-8) Circuits and their symbols.

In Figure 2-8e, two bulbs in parallel are connected to a single D-cell. How does the brightness of these bulbs compare with one another? With the brightness of the bulb in *a?* What do you think will happen if you remove one of the bulbs from its holder? Will the other bulb continue to shine or will it go out? Try it! Were you right? Can you explain why these bulbs behave differently than the bulbs wired in series? Do you think the lights in your home are wired in series or in parallel? What makes you think so?

Finally, circuit 2-8f consists of two D-cells in series connected to two bulbs wired in parallel. How does the brightness of each of these bulbs compare with the bulb in circuit *a*? With the bulb in circuit *b*? With the bulb in circuit 2-8d?

Exploring on Your Own

- Predict how the brightness of the bulbs in each of the following circuits will compare with the brightness of the bulbs in the circuits in Figure 2-8a and b:

  Circuit 1: one bulb connected to 3 D-cells in series

  Circuit 2: one bulb connected to 3 D-cells in parallel

  Circuit 3: three bulbs in series connected to one D-cell; to 3D-cells in series

  Circuit 4: three bulbs in parallel connected to 3 D-cells in parallel

- If you can afford the cost of some D-cells, measure the time a bulb will continue to glow when connected to a single new D-cell. Now try two bulbs. If you connect the two bulbs in series, do you think they will burn longer or for less time than the single bulb you tested? What do you think their "burnout" time will be if you connect them in parallel to a single new D-cell? Test your predictions. What do you find? Can you explain your results?

- Create a short circuit by taping a bare copper wire to the terminals of a D-cell. After five minutes, feel the cell. Is it warm? Can you still light a bulb with the cell? Is the cell still warm after an hour? Will the cell still light a bulb after an hour?

- Figure 2-9 shows you how to make a simple switch that can be used to turn a bulb on and off. Using similar materials, see if you can design a two-way switch, that is, a pair of switches that enable you to turn the flashlight bulb on and off at two different locations. You probably have such switches in your home. For example, a light over a stairwell usually can be turned on and off from switches at the top and bottom of the stairs.

Just for Fun

- See how many bulbs wired in series you can light using just one D-cell.

- Make an electrical quiz board like the one shown in Fig. 2-10. Punch two sets of small, equally spaced holes through a heavy sheet of

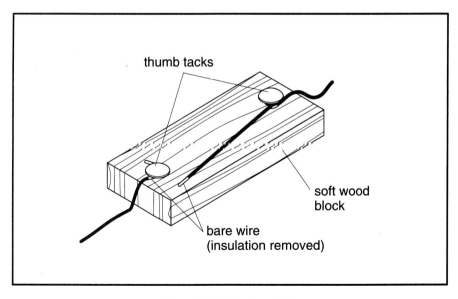

Figure 2-9) A simple switch.

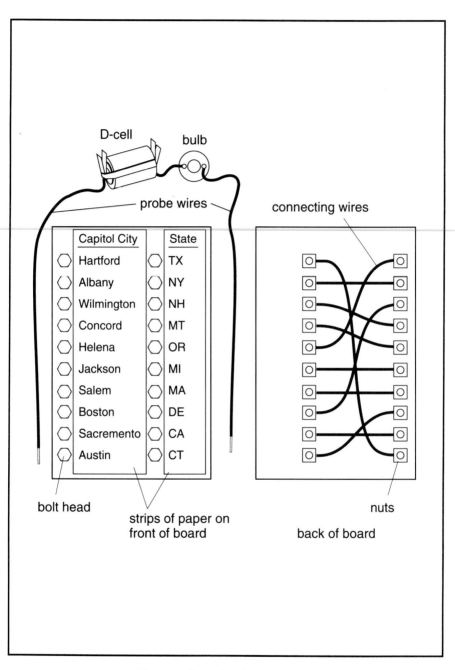

Figure 2-10) An electrical quizboard.

cardboard. Push the shaft of a small, short, threaded bolt through each hole. Now paste a strip of paper beside each row of bolt heads. On one strip of paper make a list of names of things that are to be matched with a second list of names on the other strip. In Fig. 2-10, states are to be matched with capital cities, but any matching items could be used—animals and their footprints, nations and their populations, presidents and their political parties, and so on. Now turn the sheet of cardboard over and put the nuts on the bolts. Before you tighten the nuts, run strips of insulated wire along the back side of the cardboard sheet connecting the bolts with the matching information. The bared ends of these wires are held in place by the nuts. Tighten the nuts by hand and turn the sheet over. Add a bulb, D-cell, and probe wires and your quiz-study board is ready. The person taking the quiz touches the bolt head beside the name on one list with one of the wires and uses the second wire to touch the bolt head beside the matching word on the other list. If you have wired the back of the sheet correctly, the light will go on only if the correct match is made.

Electric Charge

Is there any connection between the positive and negative charges produced by rubbing plastic, glass, rubber, and other materials with wool, silk, and paper and the positive and negative terminals found on batteries? Figure 2-11 shows that there is indeed a connection. Experiments too dangerous for you to perform indicate that when the positive terminal of a high-voltage battery is connected to the top and the negative terminal to the side of an electroscope, there is a charge on the electroscope leaves. The electroscope behaves in the same way that it does when it is touched with a positively charged rod. If we bring a glass rod that has been rubbed with silk near the top of the electroscope, the leaves move farther apart, showing that the charge on the leaves is positive.

If the battery connections are reversed so that the negative terminal is connected to the leaves through the top of the electroscope, the leaves come together when a positively charged rod is brought near the top. The positive charge, therefore, must be attracting an opposite charge from the leaves to the top of the scope. The leaves must have been carrying a negative charge.

Such experiments show that a battery can separate charges. Positive charges collect at one pole or terminal and negative charges at the other. The charges separated by a battery have the same properties as

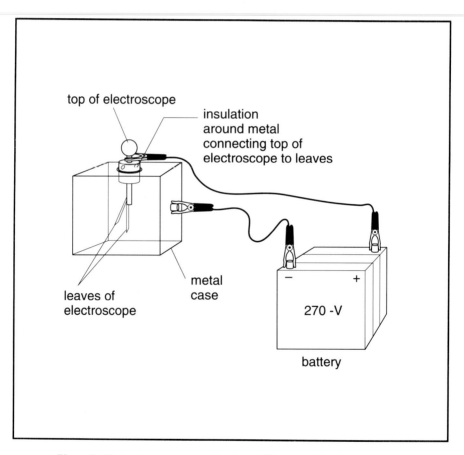

Figure 2-11) An electroscope can be changed by connecting it to a battery.

the charges produced by rubbing materials (see chapter 1). If you connect one terminal of a battery to a light bulb (or some other electrical device) and the other side of the bulb to the other terminal of the battery, charges flow from one terminal to the other through the bulb. Such an experiment does not, however, indicate whether positive charge, negative charge, or both kinds of charge flow through the circuit.

A Model for Electric Circuits

In all the circuits you have built, one thing is quite clear—unless the circuit is connected to both the positive and negative terminals of a battery, nothing happens. This observation gave rise to a theory that attempts to explain electric circuits. Electric charge—the stuff that we call electricity—moves from one pole of a battery to the other. It passes through bulbs, wires, and motors that are connected between the two poles of the battery. If a circuit divides, as in a parallel circuit, some of the charge goes through one branch and the rest goes through the other branch.

Early scientists thought that electric charge was like a fluid that flowed from one side of the battery to the other. Later, charge was believed to consist of tiny particles that moved through circuits. Regardless of what charge is, whether it moves through a circuit depends on what is used to connect the circuit to the battery. If you use metal wires to connect a bulb to the poles of a battery, the bulb lights. If you connect the bulb to the battery with cloth or plastic fibers, nothing happens. We will investigate the ability of different materials to conduct (move) charge through circuits in the next chapter.

3

Conductors, Nonconductors,
and Resistors

Flashlight bulbs connected to a battery or household bulbs connected to lines from a power company will not work unless the charge can move through the circuit. The amount of charge that flows in a given time is called electric current. Most electrical devices require an electric current if they are to work. However, some devices require a very large current, that is, a lot of charge must flow through them in a given time; others require a very small current. In this chapter, you will find out how to control charge flow. You will also see that materials differ in the amount of charge that will move through them.

3.1 Conductors and Nonconductors*

In this experiment, you will look at a variety of materials to decide which ones can conduct electric current and which ones can't.

To find out if something is a conductor, you can build the incomplete circuit shown in Figure 3-1a (both a detailed circuit and one using symbols are provided). What you use for bulb and battery holders will depend on what you did in the Bulb and Battery Holders experiment in Chapter 2. Connect the three D-cells in series. Then con-

Things you'll need:

- D-cells
- wires
- battery holders
- variety of materials—nails, plastic, pencil and pencil lead, silverware, wood, paper, coins, candle wax, chalk, etc.
- flashlight bulb (If possible, use a GE #48 bulb when testing liquids.)
- bulb holder

nect a wire to each end of the battery. One of these wires should be connected to a bulb. The second will be used to touch one side of the object to be tested. Connect a third wire to the other side of the bulb. It will be used to touch the other side of the object being tested.

Firmly, but just for a moment, touch the object you are testing with the ends of the two wires. (If you touch for too long, you might burn out the bulb.) If the bulb lights, what does it tell you about the object's ability to conduct charge? What do you know if the bulb does not light?

Test the various materials listed. Which ones are conductors? Which appear to be nonconductors?

From your tests, can you explain why rubber bands were used for making battery holders (see Figure 2-6a, b, and c)? What would happen if the rubber bands were replaced by metal straps? Why were Fahnestock clips, paper clips, or metal tabs used to make contact with the poles of the battery? Could you have used cardboard tabs instead?

Now test the various parts of a flashlight or household bulb. Do you think the metal side of the bulb is a conductor? How about the

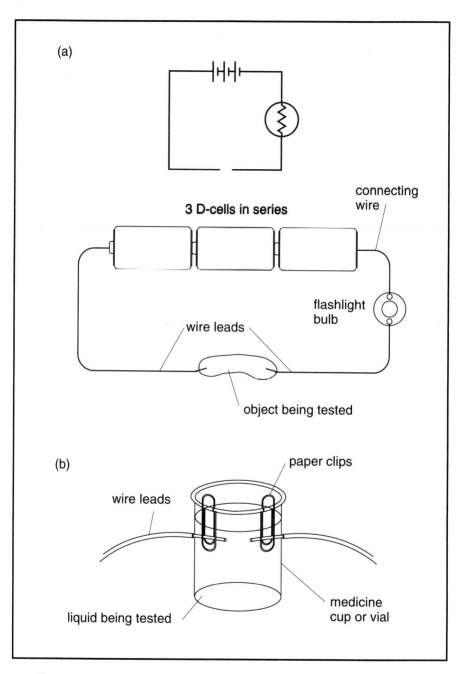

(a)

3 D-cells in series

connecting wire

flashlight bulb

wire leads

object being tested

(b)

paper clips

wire leads

liquid being tested

medicine cup or vial

Figure 3-1a) Testing solids for conductivity. b) Testing liquids for conductivity.

small metal knob at the bottom of the bulb? The ceramic material around the metal knob? How do you know that the bulb's filament is a conductor? Can you explain now why you have to touch certain places to make a bulb light?

Which parts of the outside of a D-cell will conduct charge? Does it depend on the brand of D-cell?

Exploring on Your Own

Do you think any liquids will conduct electric charge? To find out, place the liquid you want to test in a medicine cup or vial. Slide two paper clips over the sides of the container as shown in Figure 3-1b. At least the lower half of the side of each clip that is within the cup should be covered with liquid. Slide one lead wire under the part of one paper clip that is outside the cup. Then, after checking to be sure the two paper clips are not in contact, touch the other paper clip with the second lead wire.

Test a number of different liquids. If the bulb lights, what does this tell you about the liquid you are testing?

If the bulb does not light, perhaps the liquid is a nonconductor, or it may be a poor conductor. Do you see gas bubbles forming around either of the paper clips? The bubbles show that even though there is not enough electric current to light the bulb, there is enough to cause some kind of chemical reaction around the electrodes (paper clips). Will the bulb light if you connect four, five, or six cells in series to the liquids that are poor conductors? (**For reasons of safety, don't exceed six D-cells in series.**)

3.2 Wire Length and Resistance to Charge Flow*

From your results in Chapter 2, you know that two flashlight bulbs in series do not glow as brightly as a single bulb. This suggests that two bulbs in series resist the flow of charge more than a single bulb. Perhaps the resistance to charge flow is related to the very thin wires that make up the filaments in the bulbs. If we connect two identical bulbs in series, we have doubled the length of the filaments in the circuit. Could it be that the length of a wire affects the wire's resistance to the flow of charge? This experiment will give you an opportunity to find out.

To see how the length of a wire affects its resistance to the flow of electric charge, you can build the circuit shown in Figure 3-2. Use two thumbtacks to secure the ends of a piece of the #30 nichrome

Things you'll need:

- thumbtacks
- 2 feet (60 cm) of #30 (thin) Nichrome (chromel) wire (your school's science lab probably has some)
- piece of cardboard or soft wood
- wires
- D-cells
- battery holder(s)
- flashlight bulb
- bulb holder
- 2 feet (60 cm) of #26 (thick) Nichrome (chromel) wire
- 6 feet (2 m) of #26 or #28 bare copper wire (You can buy at a hardware or electronics store or borrow from your school's science lab.)

(chromel) wire to a piece of cardboard or soft wood. The bare end of wire 1 in Figure 3-2, which connects the D-cell to the nichrome wire, should also be under the thumbtack shown at the left side of the drawing. Wire 2 connects the D-cell to the flashlight bulb. Wire 3 connects the flashlight bulb to the other side of the nichrome wire. To start, hold the end of wire 3 on the thumbtack at the left end of the nichrome wire. The bulb should light as it did in Figure 2-8a because the nichrome wire is not yet part of the circuit.

Now move the end of wire 3 slowly along the nichrome wire from left to right as shown in the drawing. What happens to the brightness of the bulb? Does the nichrome wire appear to offer more resistance to charge flow as its length included in the circuit increases? What length of nichrome wire is needed to turn off the bulb?

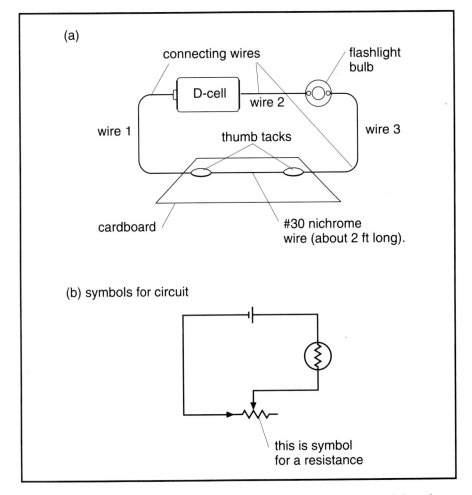

Figure 3-2) How does the length of a wire affect its resistance to the flow of charge?

Now connect the bulb to two D-cells. Do you think a greater or a lesser length of wire will be needed to turn off the bulb this time? Try it! Were you right?

Next, build a circuit with one D-cell and two light bulbs in series. What length of wire do you think will be needed to turn off both bulbs? Try it and see how closely your prediction agrees with the experiment.

Based on the experiments you have done, how does the length of a nichrome wire affect its resistance to the flow of electric charge?

Repeat the experiment with a similar length of thicker (#26) nichrome wire. How does the thickness of a wire appear to affect its resistance to the flow of charge?

Finally, repeat the experiment using a long piece of bare copper wire that is about the same diameter as one of the nichrome wires you used. Can you put out the bulb with two feet of this copper wire? With four feet? Six feet?

Does the kind of metal in a wire affect its resistance? (We'll assume from now on that *resistance* means resistance to the flow of charge.)

Exploring on Your Own

- Cut a length of thin (#30) nichrome wire just long enough to turn off a bulb when wired in series with the bulb. Insert the wire into the circuit as you did before (Figure 3-2). Now reduce the length of the wire in the circuit until the bulb glows dimly. What do you think will happen to the brightness of the bulb if you connect a second piece of identical nichrome wire in parallel with the first one? Hint: Remember how the thickness of a wire affects its resistance to charge flow. What do you find? Was your prediction correct? What do you think will happen to the brightness of the bulb if you add a third wire in parallel with the other two? Were you right?

- Build the two circuits shown in Figure 3-3. As you know, the brightness of the bulb will decrease as you lengthen the nichrome wire in series with the bulb in circuit 3-3a. What do you think will happen to the brightness of the bulb as you increase the length of the nichrome wire in circuit 3-3b? Test your prediction experimentally. How do you explain your results?

- Try to predict which of the bulbs will light in the circuits shown in Figure 3-4. Then test your predictions. Were all your predictions

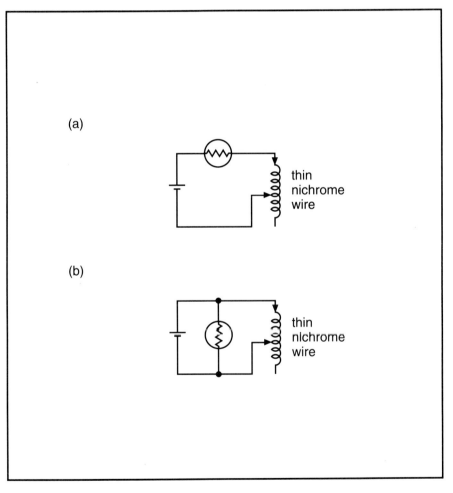

Figure 3-3) Two nichrome wire circuits.

(a)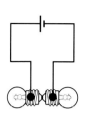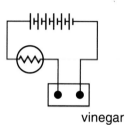

(b)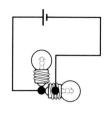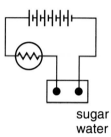

(c)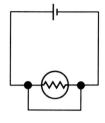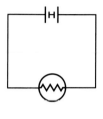

(d)

vinegar

(e)

sugar water

(f)

(g)

paper tube

(h)

24 inches of thin nichrome wire

(i)

(j)

24 inches of thin nichrome wire

(k)

hammer with wooden handle

(l)

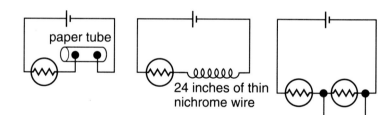
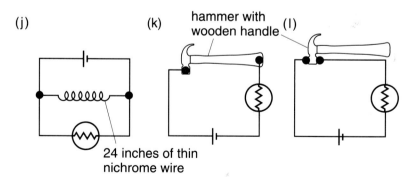

Figure 3-4) In which of these circuits will the bulb(s) light?

correct? If possible, discuss your predictions with others who have tried the same experiments.

- From what you know about the conductivity of water and copper wire, what do you think will happen if you lower a glowing bulb attached to a D-cell into a glass of water. Try it. Were you right? Will it make any difference if you use salt water?

Superconductors

It has been known for some time that at very low temperatures (temperatures close to -273°C) some materials become superconductors. That is, they offer no resistance to the flow of charge. More recently, a compound containing copper, barium, oxygen and yttrium was found to become a superconductor at temperatures slightly above the boiling point of liquid nitrogen (-196°C). While such a temperature is still very cold, it is much easier to achieve than -273°C. And liquid nitrogen is a relatively inexpensive material. Consequently, it may be possible to design electrical motors and other electrical devices using superconductors that will operate at the temperature of liquid nitrogen. By using superconductors, resistance is greatly reduced and less electrical energy is needed to power motors and other devices. It is hoped that in the future substances will be developed that will be superconducting at room temperature. Such materials would require none of the special cold conditions required for superconductors today. The increased efficiency made possible by superconductors could lead to a number of technological breakthroughs in transportation, communications, and computers.

3.3 Making a Light Bulb

In the experiments you have done, you have seen that thin wires have more resistance than thick wires. You have seen too that Nichrome wires have more resistance than similar wires made of copper. In fact, most metals are better conductors than Nichrome, that is, they offer less resistance to the flow of

Things you'll need:

- bare, thick copper wires
- clay
- D-cells
- short length of thin (#30) Nichrome wire
- battery holders

charge. Nichrome wires have a resistance that is about sixty times greater than comparable wires made of copper.

The wires that make up the filaments in flashlight bulbs are very thin. This suggests that the resistance of these wires is quite high. When electric current is "blocked," some of the electrical energy is changed into heat. If the resistance is high enough, the heat may be so intense that the wire glows like a hot wood fire. This is why high-resistance wires are used in light bulbs. The wires in the bulb that support the filament and connect it to the circuit are quite thick. These wires offer little resistance to the flow of charge. When you build a bulb of your own in this experiment, you will use Nichrome wire in the filament and thick copper wires to connect the filament to the battery.

Over 100 years ago, Thomas Edison found that filaments will burn up if heated by electricity in air. On the other hand, in a vacuum, the filament quickly evaporates when heated. As a result, air is removed from light bulbs and partially replaced with argon and/or nitrogen gas. Filaments do not burn up or evaporate in such an atmosphere and will last a long time.

Build the "bulb" shown in Figure 3-5 by supporting two thick pieces of copper wire upright with a piece of clay as shown. The two upright copper wires supported by clay should be about 1/4 inch (6 mm) apart. Wrap the ends of a short piece of thin Nichrome wire firmly around the ends of the two copper wires. This is the filament of your bulb. Now connect the copper wires to the poles of a D-cell supported by a battery holder. Do not touch the filament, it will be hot. Does the filament glow? If it does not, connect another D-cell in series with the first one. How is this bulb similar to a regular flashlight bulb? How is it different?

Save this setup. You can use it in the next experiment where you will build a fuse.

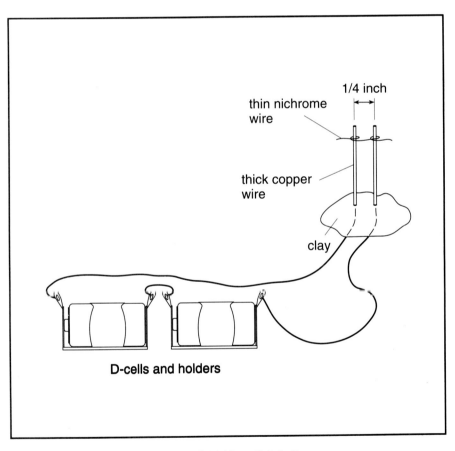

Figure 3-5) Making a light bulb.

3.4 Making a Fuse

A fuse is an electrical device that is designed to burn out when a circuit carries too much current. If a short circuit were to develop in a circuit (see "A Second Wire" in Chapter 2), there would be very little resistance in the circuit. The large current that would then flow could produce a lot of heat and

Things you'll need:

- bulb made in preceding experiment
- short lengths of wire from a pad of steel wool
- flashlight bulb
- bulb holder
- connecting wires

cause a fire. The fuse, by burning out, breaks the circuit and prevents excessive heat from developing.

Remove the nichrome wire "filament" from the bulb you built in the preceding experiment. Replace it with a single short piece of wire from a pad of steel wool. The thin steel wire serves as a fuse in this circuit. When you connect the circuit to two D-cells in series, you will see what happens to a fuse when there is a short circuit.

Now let's see how a fuse works in a typical circuit. Rebuild the circuit, but this time place a flashlight bulb in series with the fuse. When you connect the circuit this time, the fuse should not blow. The bulb has a resistance that restricts the flow of charge. With less charge flowing through the fuse, it does not get hot enough to melt. (If it does melt, use one D-cell instead of two and repeat the experiment.)

To see what happens when a short circuit occurs, place a thick, bare copper wire in parallel with the bulb. That is, firmly touch both ends of a short piece of copper wire to the connections leading to the bulb as shown in Figure 3-6. Is the resistance of the copper wire large or small? What happens to the fuse?

Exploring on Your Own

- Hold your hand near (but don't touch) an incandescent light bulb that is emitting light. In addition to light, what else is produced when electric charges flow through a light bulb?

- Look carefully at the bulb used in the taillight of a car. (You can buy such a bulb in an auto supply store.) How many filaments are in the bulb? Are all of the filaments the same? Can you predict which one will glow more brightly? Now see if you can light each filament separately with a battery made of D-cells. Were you right about the brightness? Can you light both filaments at the same time?

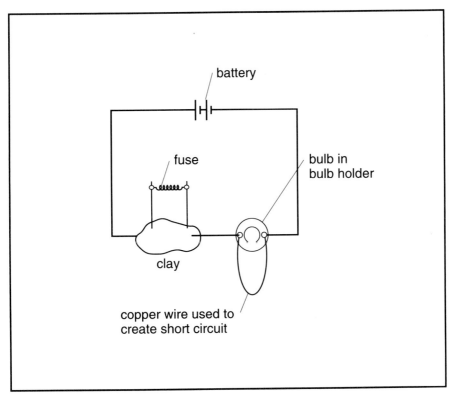

Figure 3-6) Making a short circuit with a fuse in place.

Why does a car taillight have more than one filament? Can you guess what purpose each filament has?

You have seen that some materials, called electrical conductors, allow electric charge to flow through them. Other materials, such as the ceramic that separates the terminals of a flashlight or household bulb or the plastic around an insulated wire, are nonconductors or insulators. Still other materials, such as solutions of vinegar or ammonia, are weak conductors of electricity. There are also solids, such as arsenic and germanium, that are weak conductors of electricity. They are called semiconductors.

In building circuits, conductors are used to carry charge and nonconductors to prevent the flow of charge. A plastic-covered copper wire is a good conductor surrounded by a nonconductor. Such an insulated wire helps prevent short circuits. If bare copper wires were used in circuits, a conductor might touch the copper on both sides of a bulb, causing a short circuit.

Many circuits contain fuses in series with the rest of the circuit. When a large current flows through the circuit, the fuse melts. Such large currents may result from a short circuit or from someone's failure to place a sufficiently large resistance in the circuit. As you have seen, the filaments in light bulbs and other thin wires resist the flow of electric charge. By connecting bulbs in series, you can increase the resistance of a circuit. On the other hand, bulbs wired in parallel offer less resistance to charge flow. Two bulbs side by side has the same effect as making the filament of one bulb thicker. As a result, the total current through two bulbs in parallel is approximately double the current through a single bulb.

Now that you know how to build circuits and understand the symbols used to represent these circuits, you can return to a question that was raised earlier. How are electricity and magnetism related? You will explore that question in Chapter 4.

4

The Link Between Electricity and Magnetism

For centuries, people thought that electricity and magnetism were somehow related, but no one could find any connecting link between them. Then, in 1819, Hans Christian Oersted, a Danish physicist, discovered the connection quite by accident when he brought a magnetic compass near a wire that was carrying electric current. By doing this next experiment, you can make the same discovery that Oersted made.

4-1 Oersted's Discovery*

Put a magnetic compass on a table or counter. Place a long insulated wire on top of the compass. Be sure the wire is nearly parallel to the compass needle as shown in Figure 4-1a. Connect one end of the wire

Things you'll need:
- 2 to 3 D-cells
- long insulated wire
- magnetic compass

to a battery of two or three D-cells in series. Then briefly touch the other end of the wire to the other terminal of the battery. What happens to the compass needle? What does this tell you about the connection between an electric current and magnetism?

Place the wire beneath the compass and repeat the experiment. What do you notice this time? What is different? What is the same?

Again, place the wire above and parallel to the compass needle, but this time reverse the connections and the current by touching the ends of the wire to the opposite terminals of the battery. What do you observe this time when a charge flows through the wire?

The Magnetic Field Around a Current

Figure 4-1b shows a long, straight vertical wire whose ends are connected to the opposite poles of a battery. Since the wire forms a short circuit across the battery, there is a large current in the wire. As you can see from the compasses placed around the wire, the magnetic lines of force (the magnetic field) form a circular pattern around the current. Does this agree with what you found when a current flowed above or below a magnetic compass?

Exploring on Your Own

- Using a long piece of insulated wire, a battery consisting of four to eight D-cells, and a cardboard platform supported by chairs, build the circuit shown in Figure 4-1b. Because this is a short circuit, do

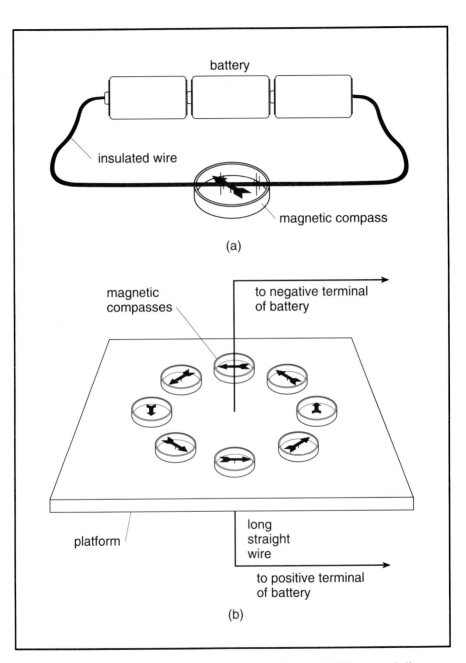

Figure 4-1a) An experiment that leads to Oersted's dicovery. b) The magnetic lines of force or field around a current in a wire.

not leave it connected for very long. You may not have a large number of compasses. However, you can easily move one compass around the wire to see if the magnetic lines of force form a circular pattern like the one seen in Figure 4-1b. Or you can sprinkle iron filings or small pieces of steel wool on the cardboard. As you know, each of the filings acts like a tiny compass needle. Tap the cardboard and see if the filings form a circular pattern around the current in the wire.

4-2 A Magnet from Electricity*

Oersted's discovery made people realize that magnets could be produced with electric currents. In France, André Ampère showed that the magnetic effects produced by electricity could be used to measure electric current. In this experiment and the next, you will see how an electric current can be used to make a magnet and how this electrically made magnet can be used to detect an electric current.

Things you'll need:

- D-cells
- battery holder
- tape
- magnetic compass
- 24 feet of #24 enamel-coated copper wire
- wire cutting pliers
- sandpaper

Cut a 24-foot length of enamel-coated wire in half. (The enamel on the wire insulates it so you can wind the wire into a coil without producing a short circuit.) Wind each of the two lengths of wire into a coil. This can be done by wrapping the wire around a D-cell as shown in Figure 4-2a. Use two small pieces of tape to hold the coils in place (Fig. 4-2b). Leave about a foot of wire uncoiled at each end. These straight wires will be used as leads to connect the coil to a D-cell. However, since the wires are insulated, use sandpaper to remove about an inch of enamel from each end of the leads to the coil as shown in Fig. 4-2c.

Now attach the two ends of the wire from one coil to a D-cell as shown in Figure 4-3 so charge can flow through the coil. Do not leave the coil connected longer than necessary or you will wear out the D-cell. Let the coil hang from the cell while you or a partner move a magnetic compass in the vicinity of the coil. Does the coil behave like a magnet? Which side of the coil is the north-seeking pole?

Attach the second coil to another D-cell. Does it too behave like a magnet? What do you think will happen if you hold the faces of these coils close to one another? Can you make the coils repel one another? Can you make them attract one another?

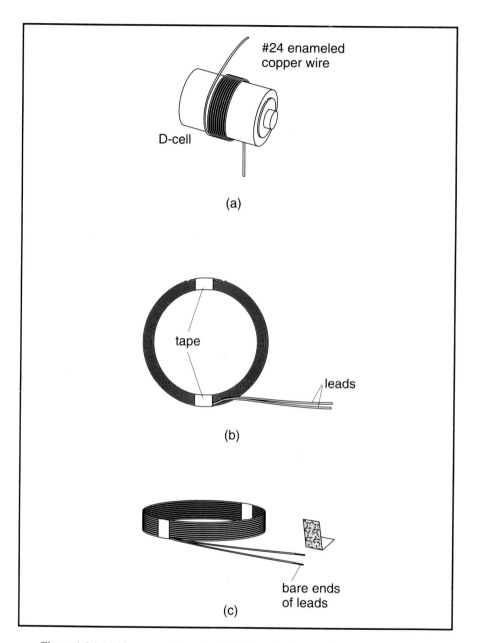

Figure 4-2a) Making magnetic coils. Wind the wire into a coil on a D-cell. b) Use tape to hold the wires together. c) Use sandpaper to remove enamel from the ends of the wire leads.

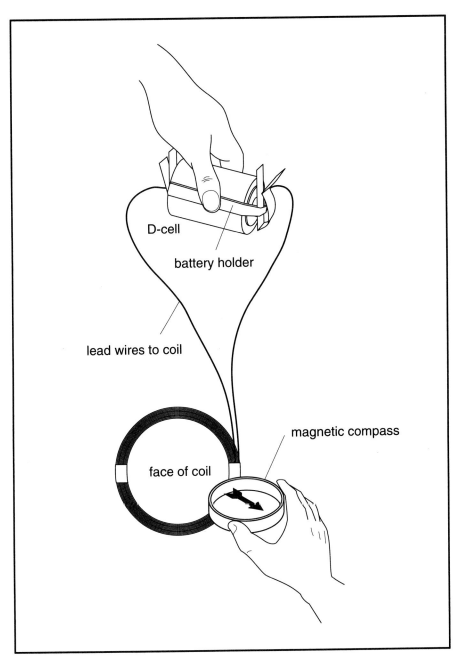

Figure 4-3) Testing a coil for magnetism.

4-3 An Electric Current Detector*

Ampère found that he could use a coil of wire and a magnet to detect and measure an electric current. To see how he did this, place a compass inside one of the coils you made during the preceding experiment. You may want to use a little clay to hold the coil and compass in place as shown in Figure 4-4. (If your coil does not fit around the compass, unwrap it and build another by wrapping the enameled wire around (over and under) the compass. Be sure the wires in the coil are parallel with the compass needle and that the needle is free to turn.

Things you'll need:
- D-cell
- battery holders
- tape
- magnetic compass
- 24 feet of #24 enamel-coated copper wire
- sandpaper
- coils from preceding experiment
- clay
- flashlight bulb
- bulb holder

What happens to the compass needle when you connect the leads from the coil to a D-cell? (Do not connect the coil to the D-cell for long or you will wear out the cell.) The device you have built is called a galvanoscope. It can be used to detect very small currents.

How much is the needle deflected by the current from a D-cell? Place a flashlight bulb in series with the coil. Do you think the deflection of the needle will be more or less with a bulb in the circuit? Test your prediction. Were you right? What will happen to the deflection of the needle if you place two bulbs in series with the coil? Three? Four?

If you connect enough bulbs in series, you will reach a point where none of the bulbs will light. Does the galvanoscope still detect an electric current even when none of the bulbs light?

Exploring on Your Own

• Make two coils that will fit around a magnetic compass. Make one coil with ten turns of wire; make the other with fifty turns. Test both galvanoscopes with a circuit that contains several bulbs in series with the coil. With which coil does the compass needle deflect more? How would you build a galvanoscope that would detect smaller currents than those you can detect with any of your present galvanoscopes?

• Suppose the compass needle of your galvanoscope is perpendicular to the wires in the coil instead of parallel to them. What will happen to the needle when charge flows through the coil?

• Suspend two coils from D-cells as you did in the preceding experiment. With the coils close together and the north-seeking poles of the coils facing each other, start one coil swinging back and forth. What happens to the other coil? See if you can explain what you observe.

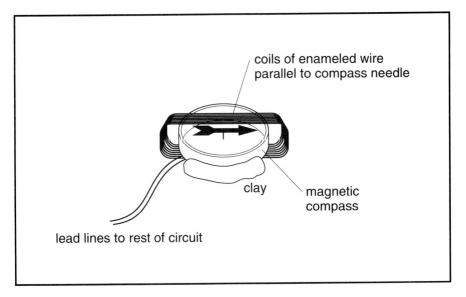

Figure 4-4) A galvanoscope.

4-4 An Electromagnet*

Early in the nineteenth century, the English scientist, William Sturgeon, found that the strength of a magnet made from a coil of wire could be increased by placing a soft iron core in the center of the coil. The magnetic lines of force appeared to become concentrated in the iron. Sturgeon was able to lift a nine-pound weight with his electromagnet, which itself weighed

Things you'll need:

• common nail

• a few feet of enameled copper wire

• sandpaper

• paper clips

• D-cells

• battery holders

only a pound. To better understand the workings of an electromagnet, you can make one of your own.

Try to lift a paper clip by touching it with a nail. Is it possible?

Now make an electromagnet by wrapping about fifty turns of enameled copper wire around the nail as shown in Fig. 4-5. Always wrap the wire in the same direction. Leave about a foot of wire at each end of the coil to connect a D-cell. Use sandpaper to remove the insulating enamel from the ends of the wire. Why must you use insulated wire to make the coil?

Connect the two ends of the wire to the terminals of a D-cell. (Do not connect these wires to the cell for very long or you will wear out the cell.) How many paper clips end-to-end can you lift with the nail now? What happens to the paper clips when you disconnect the electromagnet from the D-cell? Can you lift more paper clips if you connect the electromagnet to two D-cells? To three D-cells?

Unwind about twenty-five turns of wire from the coil. How many paper clips can you lift with half as many turns in the coil? Does the number of turns of wire around the nail affect the strength of the electromagnet?

See if you can predict the number of paper clips you can lift with 100 turns of wire around the nail. Then try it. How closely does your prediction agree with the actual number lifted?

Exploring on Your Own

- Design an experiment to find out whether the size of the iron core affects the strength of an electromagnet. Then carry out your experiment. What do you find?

- Build an electromagnet using a pencil rather than a nail as the core. How does the strength of this electromagnet compare with the one that uses an iron nail?

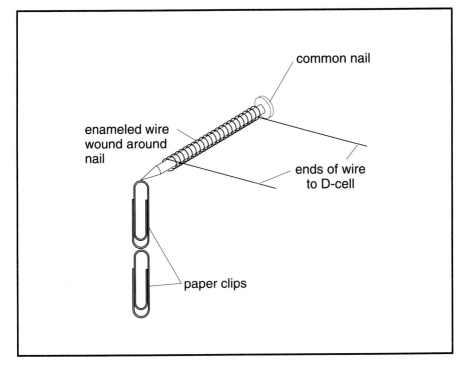

Figure 4-5) An electromagnet.

- Can other metals, such as aluminum, copper, and brass be substituted for iron as a core for an electromagnet? Design and carry out an experiment to find out. What do the results of your experiment tell you?

- Can other types of wire, such as aluminum, iron, and Nichrome, be used to make the coil for an electromagnet? Design and carry out an experiment to answer this question.

- Build an electromagnet in which you wind twenty-five turns of the coil in one direction and twenty-five turns in the opposite direction. How strong is this magnet? Can you explain why?

4-5 Simple Electric Motors*

One of the most common electrical devices is the electric motor. You find it in lots of places—vacuum cleaners, refrigerators, dish washers, clothes washers, electric dryers, and other appliances. The electric motor, which has literally changed households throughout the world, is based on the interaction of magnets and electricity.

It was Michael Faraday who in 1821 built the world's first electric motor. Faraday had seen the circular pattern of magnetic lines of force around the current in a wire. He reasoned that if the pole of a magnet were placed beside an electric current, the lines of force would push the pole of the magnet in a circle around the current.

Faraday proceeded to test his idea by building the simple motor shown in Figure 4-6. A stiff wire entered the mercury-filled container at the center of its top surface. Electric charge flowed from the battery into the wire and then through the liquid mercury to another wire that entered the bottom of the container. This second wire was connected to the other terminal of the battery. Sure enough, when charge flowed, Faraday saw the free end of the magnet move around the wire. Faraday built a second motor in which the magnet was fixed and one end of the wire was free to move. As Faraday expected, the wire in this motor revolved about the fixed magnet when current flowed.

Things you'll need:

- magnetic compass with metal frame
- 2 D-cells
- battery holders
- wires
- flat, square or round, ceramic or rubberized magnet
- ruler
- tape
- two 4-in (10-cm) lengths of heavy (#20) bare copper wire or paper clips
- 12-in (30-cm) length of enameled copper wire
- nail or pencil
- wire cutters
- soft wood block
- sandpaper
- thumbtacks

Faraday used mercury in the container because he knew this liquid was a good conductor of electricity. Unfortunately, Faraday worked with mercury all his life. We know now that mercury is a poisonous substance whose effects accumulate with age. It was probably mercury poisoning that caused Faraday to lose his memory in his later years.

This experiment will show you how to build two tiny electric motors of your own. After the experiment, you can build a larger electric motor if you would like to.

You can make a very simple electric motor using a magnetic compass with a metallic case, two D-cells in series, and two wires. Connect the two wires to opposite terminals of a two-D-cell battery. Hold the bare end of one wire against the side of the compass case.

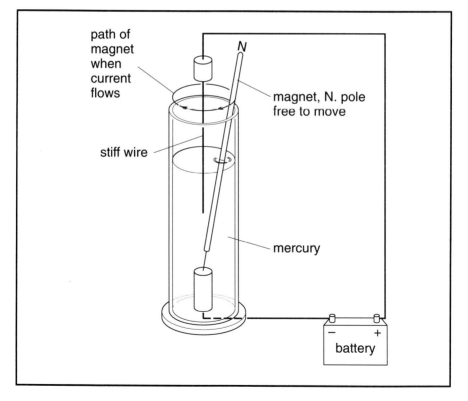

Figure 4-6) Faraday's electric motor.

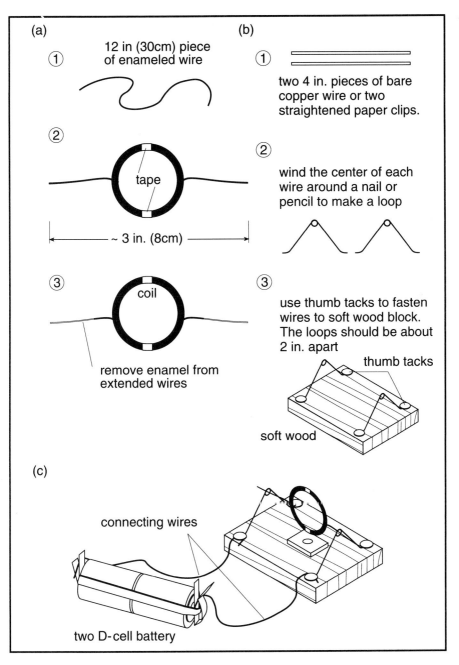

(a)

① 12 in (30cm) piece of enameled wire

② tape
— ~ 3 in. (8cm) —

③ coil
remove enamel from extended wires

(b)

① two 4 in. pieces of bare copper wire or two straightened paper clips.

② wind the center of each wire around a nail or pencil to make a loop

③ use thumb tacks to fasten wires to soft wood block. The loops should be about 2 in. apart
thumb tacks
soft wood

(c)

connecting wires
two D-cell battery

Figure 4-7) Building a small electric motor.

Then briefly touch another place on the case with the bare end of the other wire. You should see the compass needle turn. Move the position of the two wires, keeping one firmly against the case while you briefly touch and retouch the case with the second wire again and again. You will find places where you will be able to make the magnetic compass needle spin around and around like a motor.

A slightly more complicated motor can be made by wrapping a 12-in. length of enameled copper wire four times around a ruler. Wrap the two free ends of the wire once around opposite sides of the coil and extend them straight out from the coil. See Figure 4-7a. Two small pieces of tape can be used to hold the coil wires in place. The entire length of the coil and extended wires should be about three inches (8 cm). If the wires extending from the coil are too long, snip off part of their ends with a pair of wire cutters. Use sandpaper to remove the enamel from the two wires that extend out from the coil.

Next, make supports for the coil using bare copper wire or paper clips and thumbtacks as shown in Figure 4-7b. Place the wires extending from the coil through the loops of the supports. Put a magnet beneath the coil and connect wires from the thumbtacks to a two-D-cell battery as shown in Figure 4-7c. Give the coil a little flip with your fingers and watch your motor spin.

Will the motor work if you use only one D-cell? What can you do to make the motor turn faster? What can you do to make the motor turn the other way? Can you use two magnets and make the motor turn? If so, where should you place the magnets?

Just for Fun

- Make a list of all the devices, appliances, and other places where you find electric motors.

4-6 Complex Electric Motors*

To make an electric motor that more closely resembles the kind you find in complex machines will require several hours of your time. If you enjoy building things and finding out how they work, this activity will be well worth the time.

An electric motor consists of two basic parts—the armature, which moves, and the stator, which is stationary. You can build these two parts separately and then put them together.

Begin by building the armature. The steps you will follow are labeled 4-8a through 4-8f.

(a) Wind two layers of tape around the middle 1-1/2 inches of one of the 3-1/2-inch-long common nails.

Things you'll need:

- roll of #24 enameled copper wire
- roll of electrical tape
- small wooden board (about 4 in. on a side)
- 2 tacks or thumbtacks
- 2 pieces of clay
- 4 or 5 D-cells
- magnetic compass
- 3 common nails 3-1/2 in. long
- 4 common nails 2-1/2 in. long
- 4 finishing nails 2-1/2 in. long
- pliers
- hammer

(b) Tape two of the shorter common nails together. Then tape the remaining two 2-1/2-inch nails together in the same way.

(c) Hold the centers of the two pairs of nails that you have taped together on the longer nail whose center portion you taped first. These nails should be about an inch from the head of the longer nail. Then tape the two pairs of nails to the larger common nail.

(d) Wind two full layers of the enameled wire around the nails you have taped together, leaving about six inches of wire at one end, start winding the wire around the two pairs of double nails at the point where they meet the larger nail. Always wind the wire in the same direction. Wind it out from the shaft to the end of the double nails and back to the shaft, then to the other side of the shaft, out to the end of the two pairs of nails, and then back to the shaft, making a double layer of wire. Extend the wire another six inches beyond the final turn and then cut the wire at that point.

(e) Using sandpaper, carefully remove *all* the enamel insulation from the two 6-inch ends of the wire. Then fold the ends of the wire as shown. If you have too much wire, cut a little from each end.

(f) Use narrow strips of tape to fasten the two lengths of folded wire to opposite sides of the shaft. This part of the armature is called the commutator. It will be used to make an electrical connection between the armature and the stator.

Set the armature aside while you build the stator. The stator in this motor is a U-shaped electromagnet that will interact with the rotating armature. The steps you will follow are labeled g through i in Figure 4-8.

(g) Use pliers (and a vise if you have one) to bend the other two longer nails as shown. The bend should be about two inches in from the tip of the nail. If you cannot bend the nail with pliers, use a hammer to drive the nail into a one-inch-thick board to the point where you want to bend it. Then use the hammer to bend the head of the nail down onto the board. Drive the point of the nail back out of the wood and retrieve the nail.

(h) Overlap the nails as shown so that the nail heads are about three inches apart. Wrap tape around the overlapping portions of the nails to hold them together.

(i) Wrap about 400 turns of enameled wire around the nails of the stator. Again, be sure to wind all the wire in the same direction. Leave about three inches of unwound wire at each end of the coil. Sandpaper away the enamel from the last inch or so of the two 3-inch lengths of unwound wire. Two lumps of clay can be used to hold the electromagnet in place. Drive the four finishing nails into the wooden board. Position these nails so that the coil on the armature will be midway between the two poles (nail heads) of the U-shaped electromagnet.

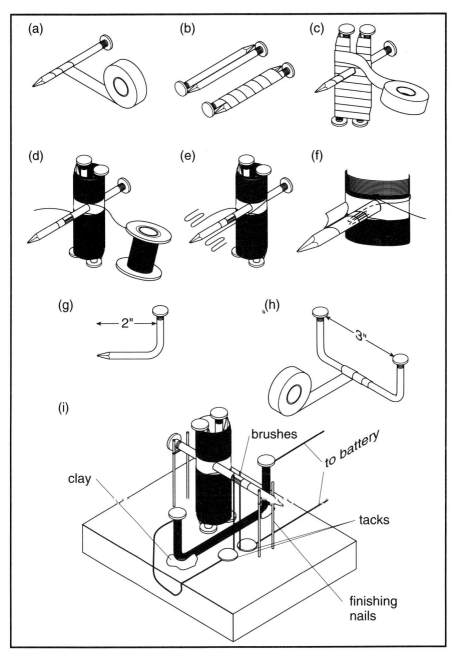

Figure 4-8) Building a sturdier electric motor.

Wrap wire around the finishing nails to support the ends of armature shaft at the same height as the poles of the electromagnet.

The last part of the stator you will make are the brushes. The brushes are used to make an electrical connection between the stator and the commutator (the wires you folded onto the shaft of the armature).

To make the brushes, sandpaper away the enamel from both ends of two 6-inch pieces of enameled wire. Use thumbtacks or tacks to fasten the wires to the board as shown in the drawing. Position the brushes so that their bare ends make solid contact with the wires on the shaft of the armature.

Use sandpaper to remove the enamel insulation from the last inch of the ends of the two wires leading to the brushes. Twist one of them tightly together with the free end of the wire that is coiled around one terminal of the U-shaped stator.

Finally, connect the other wire that leads from the brushes to one terminal of a 4-D-cell battery. Connect the other battery terminal to the bare end of the wire that emerges from the other end of the U-shaped stator. Give the armature a flip, and watch your motor spin. Adjust the tension of the brushes against the commutator until the motor runs well. Do not let the motor run for very long or you will wear out the battery.

To see how the motor works, remove the armature and hold the brushes together so electric current flows through the electromagnet alone. Use a magnetic compass to see which end of the U-shaped electromagnet is a north-seeking pole. Which is the south-seeking pole?

Now disconnect the electromagnet by separating the brushes. Connect the terminals of the D-cells to the opposite sides of the commutator so that electric charge can flow through the coil of the armature. Use the compass to locate the north-seeking pole of the armature. Where is it? Where is the south-seeking pole? Now reverse the battery connections to the commutator. You will find that the polarity of the armature also has been reversed. Can you explain why?

Replace the armature on its supports. Be sure the brushes touch the opposite sides of the commutator. Now turn the armature slowly with you fingers. You can see the connections of the battery to the armature coil are reversed every half turn. What does this do to the polarity of the coil? Can you figure out now what makes the motor turn? Hint: Remember opposite poles of two magnets or electromagnets attract and like poles repel. In the case of the motor, the magnets are the coils of the armature and stator.

What can you do to make the armature spin in the opposite direction? Will reversing the battery do it? Why or why not?

See if you can use the motor to do some useful work, such as turning a wheel or a fan.

- In the simple motor you built earlier (Figure 4-7), there was no commutator. How could the motor work without a commutator to reverse the polarity of the coil? Hint: Watch carefully as the motor turns. Does it turn smoothly, or does it bounce around?

You have seen, as Oersted did, that an electric current is surrounded by magnetic lines of force. In fact, wire wound into coils behaves like a bar magnet when charge flows through the wire. To increase the strength of such a magnet, we can insert an iron core into the coil. The iron appears to concentrate the lines of magnetic force in the metallic core. Electromagnets strong enough to lift objects weighing more than a ton can be produced when large currents flow through huge coils with soft iron cores.

Coils and magnets can also be used to make electric meters that detect even small electric currents. Coils that interact with each other and with magnets can be used to make electric motors, which are widely used in homes and industry.

5

Electricity from Magnets

All the electric lights, motors, and appliances in your home or school could be made so that they would operate by connecting them to D-cell or storage batteries, like the kind found in cars. The trouble is that it would take thousands of D-cells and scores of storage batteries to make all these things work. And you would have to replace these batteries on a daily or weekly basis.

About 150 years ago, batteries were the only way of producing a steady flow of electric charge. But in those days, there were no electric lights, motors, or other appliances. In fact, in the early 1800's, electricity was only a fascinating "toy" for scientists who were more interested in finding out what electricity was than in what it could do. Michael Faraday, upon hearing that Oersted had found that magnetic fields surround electric currents, thought that it might be possible to obtain electricity from magnets. After all, if a magnet can be made from a coil that contains moving charges, why not produce an electric current by doing something with a magnet? Faraday began by placing coils of wire near the strongest magnets he could find. But this approach proved unsuccessful. Then, in 1831, he discovered the secret. You can share in his discovery by doing the following experiment.

5-1 Electricity from Magnets*

Hold a magnet near the galvanoscope. You will see the compass needle of the galvanoscope respond to the presence of the magnet. Move the magnet farther and farther from the galvanoscope. Stop when the magnet has no effect on the galvanoscope. Now use long wires to connect the galvanoscope to a coil of wire as shown in Figure 5-1. The wire should be long enough so a magnet has no effect on a galvanoscope at this distance. The coil can be held upright with a small piece of clay.

Things you'll need:
- galvanoscope that you made in An Electric Current Detector in Chapter 4
- long wire
- coil of wire (about 2 in. [5 cm] in diameter with at least 50 turns)
- strong magnet
- clay
- electromagnet

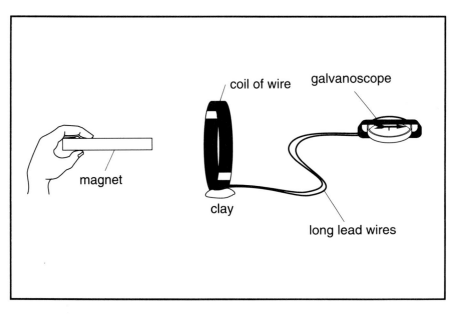

Figure 5-1) Electricity from a magnet.

To see what Faraday discovered, move the magnet in and out of the coil of wire. Watch the galavanoscope as you do this. Have you produced an electric current? How do you know? Does the speed with which you move the magnet into or out of the coil affect the size of the current?

Have a friend hold the magnet still while you move the coil over and then away from the magnet. Is a current produced? Does it matter whether it is the coil or the magnet that moves?

Hold an electromagnet inside the upright coil shown in Figure 5-1. Do you think the galvanoscope will indicate a current when you connect the electromagnet to a D-cell? Try it! Were you right? Will the galvanoscope indicate a current when you disconnect the electromagnet? What will happen if you move the electromagnet in and out of the coil while it is connected to the D-cell?

Faraday's Experiment

After many attempts to produce an electric current by placing coils near large magnets, Faraday tried an experiment that was very similar to yours. He wrapped two coils of wire around opposite sides of an iron ring. He used the iron ring because he knew, as you do, that iron concentrates the magnetic lines of force. He connected one coil to a galvanometer and the other to a battery through a switch as shown in Figure 5-2. He was delighted to find that when he turned the switch on, a momentary current was indicated by the galvanometer. A current was induced, that is, charge was "coaxed" to flow in the coil that was not connected to the battery. An induced current also flowed, but in the opposite direction, when he turned the switch off. No current flowed while the switch was on or off. Faraday realized that an induced current flowed only when the switch was being turned on or turned off.

Suddenly, he understood the secret of generating electricity from magnets. To produce a current in a coil of wire, the magnetic field through the coil must be increasing or decreasing. What was needed was not just a magnet but a magnetic field that was *changing*. Faraday tested his understanding by doing the experiment you did. When he moved the magnet into the coil, a current was indicated by the galvanometer. The increasing magnetic field through the coil caused a current. When he removed the magnet from the coil, the decreasing magnetic field through the coil caused a current to flow in the opposite direction.

We now realize why Faraday was unsuccessful in generating a current with stationary magnets regardless of their size. If it were

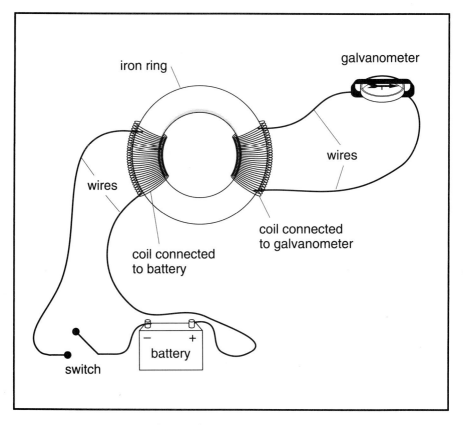

Figure 5-2) Faraday's experiment.

possible to produce electricity by just placing wires near large magnets, we would be able to light our homes and schools and turn electric motors without doing any work. Today we know that we cannot get something for nothing! We have to do work to move a magnet, or we have to use the energy inside a battery to make charges move.

Faraday built the world's first electric generator. He used a crank to turn a copper disc in the magnetic field of a large magnet as shown in Figure 5-3. As the disk turned, the changing field across the disk induced charges to flow, and he detected the charge with his galvanometer.

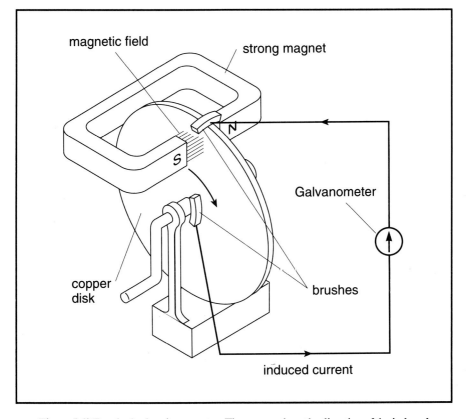

Figure 5-3) Faraday's electric generator. The arrows show the direction of the induced current.

Electric generators are found in power plants. These generators, which are turned by steam or water-powered wheels called turbines, are far larger and more complicated than Faraday's simple hand-turned model. However, the principle used to generate the electricity is based on Faraday's discovery—a changing magnetic field induces a current.

Exploring on Your Own

- If you built the electric motor shown in Figure 4-8, see if you can figure out a way to use that motor as a generator. That is, use the motor to produce electricity instead of using electricity to make the motor turn.

- Find out the various ways that electric generators are made to turn in power plants. Why are some generators located below large dams? Why are large piles of coal found near some power plants? Why are some power plants located beside nuclear reactors?

- Connect some photovoltaic cells, which convert light to electricity, to a sensitive ammeter or galvanoscope. Take your setup outside and turn the photovoltaic cells toward the sun. Can sunlight be used to produce electricity? What happens when you cover photovoltaic cells with your hand? When you turn them away from the sun? Since light from the sun is free, why don't we generate more electricity from sunlight?

- Go to a library and find out all you can about Michael Faraday. Then write your own biography of this man who may have been the greatest scientist of the nineteenth century.

Just for Fun

- Call your power company and arrange to visit one of their electric power plants.

Your Power Company's Electric Meters

At the point where the power lines enter your house, apartment, or school, you will find meters like the ones shown in Figure 5-4. The meters are read from left to right. In the meters shown in Figure 5-4, the reading is 35,169 units. The power company uses these meters to determine how much to charge you for the electrical energy they provide each month. The meters measure electrical energy in units called kilowatt-hours (kWh). For example, they might charge you ten cents for each kilowatt-hour of electrical energy they supply. However, their billing system is usually more complicated. You can read about how they determine your family's monthly charge for electricity on the back of the bill they send each month.

kilowatt-hours

Figure 5-4) Reading a power company's electric meter.

What's a Kilowatt-Hour?

As you have seen, it is possible to think of electricity as bundles of charge that move through circuits that include light bulbs, toasters, electric motors, and other appliances. Scientists have defined a single bundle of charge as a coulomb (C). Electric current is the rate at which these bundles, or coulombs, move through circuits. The units of current are called amperes (A). One ampere is equal to a charge flow of one coulomb per second (1 A = 1C/s). Each coulomb of charge carries some energy. The energy carried by each coulomb is measured in volts. One volt means that each coulomb of charge carries one joule of energy (1 V = 1J/C). A joule is not a large amount of energy. It is only enough energy to raise the temperature of one gram of water 0.24°C or 0.43°F.

Most circuits in your home or school operate at 120 volts; therefore, each coulomb of charge delivers 120 joules of energy. Suppose the current through a light bulb is 1.0 A or 1.0 C/s. The rate that energy is provided to the bulb will be 120 J/s. Since amperes, or "amps," are a measure of charge per second (current) and volts measure energy per charge (J/C), the product of these two quantities will give you the energy provided by the bulb per second. In this case,

$$1.0 \text{ A} \times 120 \text{ V} = 1.0 \text{ C/s} \times 120 \text{ J/C} = 120 \text{ J/s}$$

It is much like finding the distance you travel from time and speed. If you drive at 50 mph for two hours, you will travel 100 miles.

$$50 \text{ mi/h} \times 2 \text{ h} = 100 \text{ mi}$$

The energy provided per second is called power. It is measured in joules per second or watts (W) (1 W = 1 J/s.) Thus, the bulb in the example above was a 120-W bulb.

If a 120-W bulb is on for one hour (3,600 seconds), the energy required to operate the bulb is 432,000 J.

$$120 \text{ W} = 120 \text{ J/s}$$
$$120 \text{ J/s} \times 3,600 \text{ s} = 432,000 \text{ J}$$

		Average wattage	Average number of Appliance wattage hours used per year
Kitchen	blender	390	40
	coffee maker	900	120
	dishwasher	1200	300
	stove	12200	100
	microwave oven	1450	130
	toaster	1200	35
	refrigerator	240	3000
	refrigerator (frostless)	320	3800
Laundry	clothes dryer	4800	200
	iron	1000	140
	washing machine	500	200
	water heater	2500	1600
Comfort	air conditioner	900	1000
	electric blanket	180	830
	dehumidifier	250	1500
	humidifier	180	900
Health and beauty	hair dryer	750	50
	razor	14	80
	toothbrush	7	60
Entertainment	radio	70	1200
	TV	200	2200
Housewares	clock	2	8760
	vacuum cleaner	630	75
	sewing machine	75	140
Lighting	light bulbs (total in home)	660	1500

Table 5-1: Average wattage and usage of household appliances.

As you can see, energy is equal to power times time. If your family is using a lot of appliances, the total current through the meter where electricity enters your home might be 100 A. In one hour, the energy provided by the power company would be

$$120 \text{ V} \times 100 \text{ A} \times 3,600 \text{ s} = 43,200,000 \text{ J}$$

To avoid such large numbers, power companies measure power in kilowatts (kW) instead of watts (W). One kilowatt equals 1,000 watts (1,000W = 1.0kW) so they measure energy in kilowatt-hours (kWh). One kilowatt-hour is equal to 3,600,000 joules because

$$1 \text{ kWh} = 1,000 \text{ W} \times 3,600 \text{ s} = 1,000 \text{ J/s} \times 3,600 \text{ s} = 3,600,000 \text{ J}$$

The energy, in kilowatt-hours, needed for a 100-W bulb that is on for one hour would be

$$0.1 \text{ kW} \times 1 \text{ h} = 0.1 \text{ kWh}$$

A home that draws a current of 100 A on 120-V circuits for one hour will be charged for 12 kWh.

$$120 \text{ V} \times 100 \text{ A} = 12,000 \text{ J/s or } 12,000 \text{ W}$$
$$12,000 \text{ W} \times 1 \text{ h} = 12 \text{ kW} \times 1 \text{ h} = 12 \text{ kWh}$$

A bill for 12 kWh is certainly an easier number to use, print, and read than 43,200,000 J.

5.2 Checking Up on Your Power Company

Call your power company and ask them when they read the meters to determine your family's monthly power bill. On the day the company reads the meter, make your own

Things you'll need:
- the electric meter on your home or apartment
- power company bills

reading. Do the same thing next time they read the meter. When the electric bill arrives, compare their readings with yours. Are they about the same?

Is their charge based on the proper number of kilowatt-hours? For example, suppose that on May 1 you found the meter reading was 35,169, and on June 1, the meter reading was 36,570. For how many kilowatt-hours should they charge you?

Read the back of the bill carefully to find out how they determine the bill. Some companies charge more for the first 50 or 100 kilowatt-hours than for the rest. Some have a fuel surcharge. See if you agree with the charge found on the bill.

Power company bills are based on the number of kilowatt-hours of electrical energy that they supply. If you operate a 100-W bulb for one hour, the power company charges you for 1/10 of a kilowatt-hour (0.1 kWh) because

$$100 \text{ W} = 100\text{W}/1000 = 0.1\text{kW}$$
$$\text{and}$$
$$0.1 \text{ kW} \times 1 \text{ h} = 0.1 \text{ kWh}$$

If you operate the same 100-W bulb for ten hours, the power company will charge you for 1 kWh.

Table 5-1 contains some information about electrical appliances commonly found in homes. Which appliances require the most power to operate? Which ones are used most frequently? Which one costs the most to operate per year? Would a person save much money by not using an electric toothbrush or razor. What would be the saving in your family's electric bill if you all agreed not to watch TV for a year?

Faraday's discovery that electric charges in a coil of wire could be induced to move by a changing magnetic field eventually changed the world. It made possible the giant steam- and water-powered electric generators that provide electricity for billions of people today. You may find it difficult to imagine a world without electricity, but even a century ago, few people had access to this power source. When George Washington took the oath of office to the presidency of the United States a little more than 200 years ago, even the idea of generating electricity was unknown.

You can acquire an understanding of the history of electricity in this country by visiting the electricity exhibits at your local science museum. To realize what it was like to live without electricity, you might take a trip into the wilderness under experienced adult supervision. If possible, visit Plimoth Plantation In Plymouth, Massachusetts, Sturbridge Village in Sturbridge, Massachusetts, the old villages in Jamestown and Williamsburg, Virginia, or other such historical sites. In these communities, you may find people speaking, dressed, and living as did early American settlers in a world where electricity was unknown.

6

Electricity and Chemistry

Until Faraday's discovery that electricity could be generated by changing the magnetic field through a coil of wire, all electricity came from batteries. We still use batteries, but as we have seen, batteries cannot provide the large amounts of power needed to operate most household appliances. On the other hand, flashlights, Walkmans, or pocket radios are useless without batteries. All automobiles have battery-powered electrical systems, and electric cars are powered by batteries instead of gasoline. However, the batteries in such cars have to be connected to an electrical outlet frequently for recharging.

Electric cells all have one thing in common. Though they differ in specific contents, they are all made from chemical substances. A D-cell, for example, consists of a zinc container, which is the negative terminal, that surrounds a dark, moist mixture of manganese dioxide, powdered carbon, and ammonium chloride. A solid carbon rod runs through the center of the cell and serves as the positive terminal. A storage battery, such as the kind found in automobiles, has lead terminals immersed in a solution of sulfuric acid.

Generally, the contents of an electric cell are not very mysterious. Usually, the chemicals they contain are widely available. And as you will soon learn, electric cells are far more common than you might expect. In fact, you can easily build one for yourself.

6-1 Making a Battery*

The electric cell you are about to build might be classified as a dry cell. Actually, all dry cells are at least damp on the inside. Yours is not an exception. To reduce the mess and make clean up easy, cover a table, desk, or counter with newspaper. To prepare the terminals, use some steel wool to clean and polish one side of each of the two sheets or screens of metal, one copper and one aluminum. To prepare the material that will lie between the terminals, soak a paper towel in a jar of water. Remove the towel and sprinkle some of the cleansing powder on both its sides. The cleanser on the towel should have the consistency of a thick paste. Lay the towel on one of the metal sheets that rests, polished-side-up, on the newspaper. Place the second sheet of metal, polished-side-down, on the towel. Be sure the two metal sheets do not touch each other.

Things you'll need:

- pieces of aluminum and copper sheet metal or screening, each about 5 in. (12 cm) x 8 in. (20 cm) (The metals can be obtained from hardware or building supply stores where they are sold as flashing or screening. Roofers use the flashing to waterproof joints in roofs.)
- can of cleansing powder (Comet, Ajax, etc.)
- galvanoscope (see "An Electric Current Detector" in Chapter 4)
- water (in dish or bowl)
- wires
- flashlight bulb (#48 GE, if possible)
- alligator or Fahnestock clips
- steel wool
- newspaper
- paper towels

Now put your electric cell to work. Connect a wire to each metal sheet and then to the flashlight bulb. (Attach alligator or Fahnestock clips to the ends of the wires leading to the copper and aluminum sheets to insure good contact. If you use alligator clips, turn up one corner of the top metal sheet and connect the clips to the metal. If you use

Fahnestock clips, slide one of the clips under the lower sheet and push the other one against the top of the upper sheet.)

Now press down on the upper sheet so that the plates are squeezed firmly against the cleanser-covered towel. Be sure that the two metals touch only the towel and *not each other*.

Does the bulb light? Connect the galvanoscope to the two plates. Does it show that there is a current between the two metals?

The First Batteries: Voltaic Cells in Series

Luigi Galvani, an eighteenth-century Italian scientist who taught anatomy, found that he could make a frog's leg twitch by touching the leg with two different metals. Galvani thought that the electricity came from within the frog. He called it animal electricity. Alessandro Volta, another eighteenth-century Italian scientist, believed that the electricity came from outside the animal and had something to do with the interaction of the two different metals.

In an effort to show that electricity can be produced from two different metals, Volta became the first person to produce a continuous electric current. He built what we now call a battery by placing strips of copper and zinc in containers of salt solution as shown in Figure 6-1a. The salt solution is called the battery's electrolyte. (In the battery that you made, cleansing powder and water made up the electrolyte.) When about thirty of these electrical cells were connected in series to make a battery, a person touching the two end terminals of the battery would get a strong shock. This shock was different from any that had ever been felt before. It was not the simple one-jolt shock that you get when you touch a metal door handle after walking across a wool rug on a dry winter day. This shock was continuous because Volta had succeeded in making a device that produced a continuous flow of charge.

If wires leading from the two ends of Volta's thirty-cell battery were brought close to one another, a spark could be seen jumping the

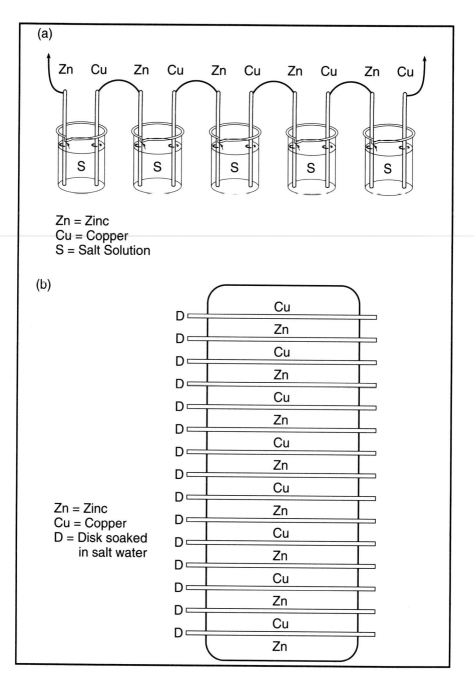

Figure 6-1) Volta's batteries: a) Metals in salt water. b) A Voltaic pile.

gap. But again, it did not end with one spark. Sparks continued to jump as long as the two wires were held near one another.

Later Volta built a more compact, less watery version of his original battery. He made a wafer-like pile consisting of a piece of zinc, a cardboard disk soaked in salt water, and a piece of copper. He repeated this layering again and again making the pile grow taller and taller. The new form of battery, which you can see in Figure 6-1b, came to be known as a Voltaic pile. Connecting the top and bottom of the pile with a wire again provided a continuous flow of charge.

6-2 Some Other Batteries*

During this investigation, you will be cleaning and handling a number of metal sheets. Your hands are likely to become dirty from the fine metal particles. **Be sure to wash your hands thoroughly each time they become dirty.**

Clean two lead plates with steel wool. Put the plates on the newspaper. Soak one of the paper towels in a jar of water and sprinkle it with some of the baking soda to make a paste on both sides of the towel. Place the towel between the two lead plates so that the plates do not touch each other. Now use two wires and clips as you did in the preceding experiment to connect the plates to the flashlight bulb. Does the bulb light when you press the top plate down against the towel? Connect the galvanoscope. Does it indicate that current is flowing?

Try charging your lead cell by connecting its plates to the opposite terminals of a two-D-cell battery for about five minutes. Then disconnect the battery and look at the surfaces of the lead plates in contact with the wet baking soda-covered paper towel. Do they look the same? Did connecting the plates to the battery change the lead plates? Will

Things you'll need:
- baking soda
- lead plates (about 4 in. [10 cm] x 6 in. [15 cm]) (Obtain from a science supply house, hardware store, or lumberyard. Lead is used for flashing on roofs.)
- paper towels
- water
- container to hold water
- newspaper
- pieces of aluminum and copper sheet metal or screening
- wires
- galvanoscope
- alligator or Fahnestock clips
- salt
- flashlight bulb (GE #48, if possible)
- bulb holder
- steel wool
- milk carton
- D-cells

the charged lead cell light a bulb? Does the galvanoscope indicate any current flow between the plates? Leave the bulb or galvanoscope connected to the lead plates until very little current flows between the plates. Then reexamine the surfaces of the lead plates. Have they changed? Can the lead cell be charged again by connecting it to D-cells?

Can you make a battery by placing a wet baking soda-covered paper towel between a clean lead plate and the aluminum sheet? Between a clean lead plate and a copper sheet? Between two copper sheets? Between two aluminum sheets?

To make still another electric cell, fill a cut-off milk carton or a beaker with a solution made from salt and water. Place an aluminum sheet into one side of the carton and a copper sheet into the other side. Be sure the two metals do not touch. Now connect a flashlight bulb (#48 GE, if possible) to the terminals of the battery. (See Figure 6-2.) Does the bulb light? Can you detect current with a galvanoscope? Make a battery from lead and aluminum sheets in the same solution. Will this battery light a bulb? Can you detect current with a galvanoscope? What about a battery made from lead and copper sheets in the same solution? Will it light a bulb? Can you detect a current?

Does the distance between the metal terminals affect the amount of current the battery produces? Does the amount of the metal submerged in the liquid affect the amount of current produced?

Can you make a battery from two sheets of the same metal?

Exploring on Your Own

- Can fruits and vegetables be used in place of paper towels and cleansing powder or salt water to make electric cells? To find out, place a copper nail and an aluminum nail or an iron nail and an aluminum nail in a lemon. (You can use strips of these metals as well as zinc in place of the nails.) Connect the two metals to a galvanoscope as shown in Figure 6-3. Does the lemon produce a current? Try some other foods, such as apples, oranges, pickles, and

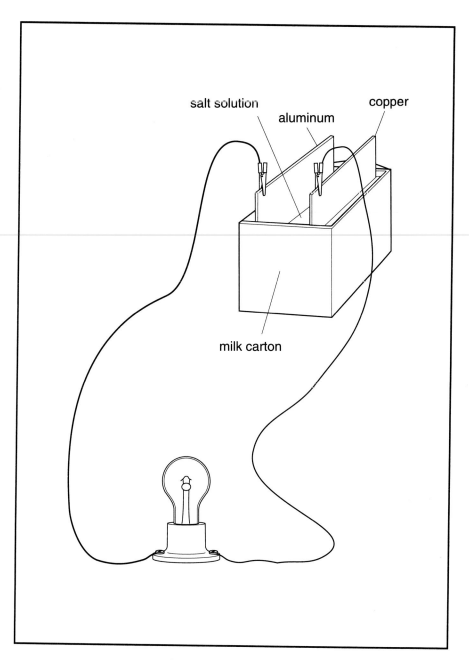

Figure 6-2) Another battery.

olives. Which combination of food and metals provides the biggest current?

Just for Fun

- Volta found that if he held strips of zinc and copper together at one end, he could feel a tingle when he put his tongue between the other ends of the two strips. Perhaps you will feel a tingle or sense a metallic taste if you place your tongue between a penny and a quarter (or between a penny and a dime) and then touch the coins together. (Be sure to wash and dry the coins before you do this.)

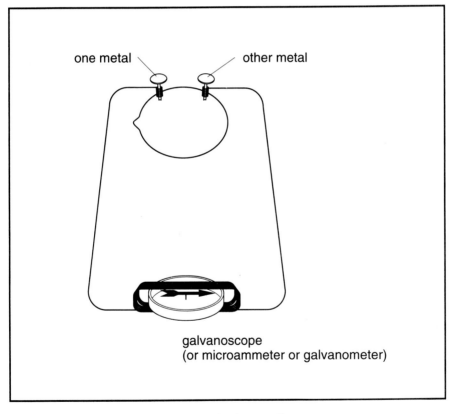

Figure 6-3) A lemon cell.

6-3 Breaking Up Water

Soon after Volta built his battery, two English scientists, William Nicholson and Anthony Carlisle, connected the terminals of a Voltaic pile to two metal rods immersed in a jar of water. You can repeat their experiment with a somewhat weaker but more convenient battery by doing this experiment.

Use the wire cutters to remove the insulation from the ends of two of the insulated copper wires. Connect the two wires to the terminals of a 6-volt dry cell battery. Place the other ends of the two wires into the clear container filled with water as shown in Figure 6-4. Be sure the wires do not touch each other. Look carefully at the surfaces of the bare ends of the immersed copper wires. You may see a few small bubbles of gas on the wires.

Things you'll need:

- water
- 6-volt dry cell battery or four D-cell battery
- insulated copper wires
- clear container
- small test tubes or clear vials
- washing soda (sodium carbonate *not* baking soda)
- wire cutters
- clay or clamps

As you remember from the "Conductors and Nonconductors" experiment in Chapter 3, water is not a very good conductor of electricity. That's why very few bubbles of gas are seen on the ends of the copper wires. To improve the conductivity of water, you can do what Nicholson and Carlisle did—add washing soda (*not* baking soda) to the water. First, remove the wires from the water, add a teaspoonful of washing soda, and stir (to dissolve the crystals faster). Replace the wires. How can you tell that the conductivity of the water has improved?

To collect the gases released at the bare ends of the wires, bend the end of each wire into a U-shape. Fill the two small test tubes or clear vials with the washing soda solution. With a finger over the open end of one tube, turn it upside down and lower its mouth below the surface of the liquid in the container. Then remove your finger. Do the same with the other tube. Pieces of clay or clamps can be used to hold the tubes in place on the sides on the container. Put the U-shaped ends of the wires under the two tubes as shown in Figure 6-5. **Do not put the U-shaped wires under the same test tube. Wash your hands; they may be sensitive to washing soda.**

The gas that bubbles off the wire connected to the positive terminal of the battery is oxygen. The gas released at the wire leading to the negative terminal is hydrogen. Let the gases collect in the tubes for a few minutes. How does the volume of hydrogen produced compare with the volume of oxygen?

Nicholson and Carlisle found that if they waited long enough they could collect measurable volumes of hydrogen and oxygen from pure water. As they suspected, when five units by volume of oxygen had collected at the wire connected to the positive terminal of the Voltaic pile, ten units of hydrogen had collected at the wire attached to the negative terminal of the same battery.

Exploring on Your Own

- Using the same setup as in this experiment, allow one of the tubes shown in Figure 6-6 to fill with hydrogen. How much oxygen can you expect to find in the other tube? **Ask an adult to help you test the two gases. Both of you should wear safety goggles.** Have the adult cover the open end of the gas-filled tube over the negative wire and lift it from the container. With the mouth of the tube pointed downward, have your adult assistant bring a thin, burning piece of wood to the mouth of the tube. If the gas burns or "pops," it is hydrogen.

Now have the adult cover the mouth of the other tube over the positive wire and remove it from the container. This time the tube should be turned so that its mouth faces upward. Have the adult lower a thin, *glowing* stick into the tube. Since oxygen makes things

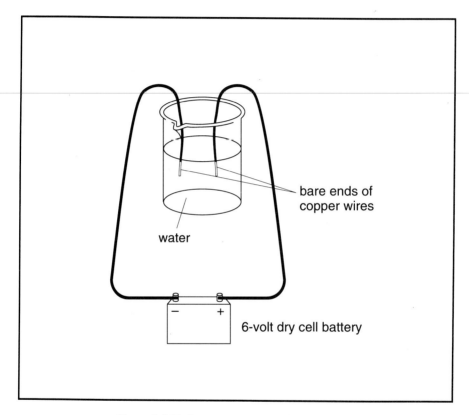

bare ends of
copper wires

water

6-volt dry cell battery

Figure 6-4) Trying to pass a current through water.

burn faster than air, what do you think will happen when the splint is placed in the tube? What does happen?

Electrolysis

The formation of hydrogen and oxygen when electricity passes through water led early chemists to suspect that Nicholson and Carlisle had succeeded in breaking water into two simpler chemicals (hydrogen and oxygen). To test this idea, these chemists mixed hydrogen and oxygen in a thick, unbreakable tube over water. When this mixture of gases was ignited by a spark, an explosion took place, practically all the gas disappeared, and water rose up the tube replacing the gases.

If the gases were ignited in a dry, sealed container, a few drops of water were all that remained after the explosion. Scientists concluded that water was a combination of hydrogen and oxygen. They also found that these two gases always combined in the same ratio—two volumes of hydrogen to one volume of oxygen. As a result when water is decomposed by electricity, two volumes of hydrogen are produced for every one volume of oxygen.

The decomposition, or breaking up, of materials by electricity came to be known as electrolysis. Thus, the decomposition of water into hydrogen and oxygen when an electric current passes through it is called electrolysis of water.

After Nicholson and Carlisle had succeeded in decomposing water by electrolysis, the English chemist Humphrey Davy used a huge battery break up solids. First he melted the solids. Then he put two carbon rods into the melt and connected them to the terminals of the battery. Davy discovered that many substances long thought to be elements, simple forms of matter made up of only one substance, could be broken down into even simpler substances. Through electrolysis, Davy was able to produce potassium from potash and sodium from soda (sodium carbonate). Using the same process, he produced four more elements—barium, strontium, calcium, and magnesium.

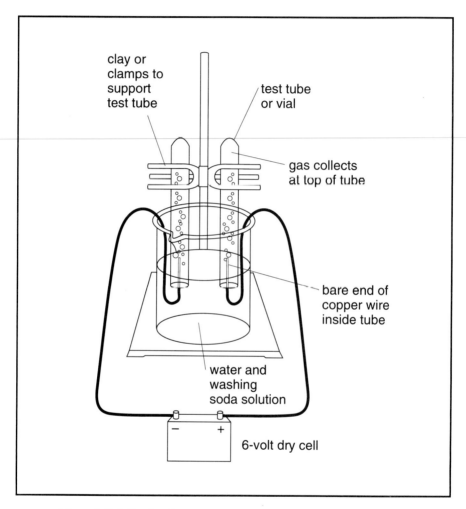

Figure 6-5) Collecting the gases produced during the electrolysis of water.

In this chapter, you have seen that electric cells can be made quite easily. All you need are two metals and an electrolyte. A very simple electric cell can be made from a copper nail, an aluminum nail, and an olive. But a good deal of engineering goes into producing an electric cell that can produce large currents, such as a dry cell or a lead storage battery.

Once Volta had succeeded in making a powerful battery, it was not long before people such as Nicholson, Carlisle, and Davy were using batteries to decompose compounds into elements.

Conclusion

By now you should have a good firsthand understanding of how electricity works. You know how to wire circuit elements, such as bulbs, in series or in parallel. You can test materials for conductivity. You know how length, diameter, and the kind of wire affect its resistance, and you know how bulbs and fuses are made.

You have seen the polarity of magnets and the fact that electric charge is either positive or negative, and you shared in Oersted's discovery that magnetic lines of force surround an electric current. You also know that a changing magnetic field will induce charges to flow in wires, which is the way the electricity we use in our homes is generated. You have seen how the interaction between electricity and magnetism makes possible electric motors and generators as well as electromagnets and current detectors.

You also know how power companies use electric meters in your house to decide how much to charge you, and you know how to check on the bills your family receives from them.

You are not an electrical engineer or an electrician yet. But if you have carried out the experiments in this book, you should have a good basic understanding of electricity and magnetism—an understanding that will help you if you pursue science in a secondary school and even in college.

Appendix:
Science Supply Companies

Carolina Biological Supply Co.
2700 York Road
Burlington, NC 27215

Central Scientific Co. (CENCO)
11222 Melrose Avenue
Franklin Park, IL 60131

Connecticut Valley Biological Supply Co., Inc.
82 Valley Road
Southampton, MA 01073

Delta Education
P.O. Box M
Nashua, NH 03061

Edmund Scientific Co.
101 E. Gloucester Pike
Barrington, NJ 08007

Educational Innovations
151 River Road
Cos Cob, CT 06807

Fisher Scientific Co.
4901 W. LeMoyne Street
Chicago, IL 60651

Frey Scientific Co.
905 Hickory Lane
Mansfield, OH 44905

McKilligan Supply Corp.
435 Main Street
Johnson City, NY 13790

Nasco Science
901 Janesville Road
Fort Atkinson, WI 53538

Nasco West Inc.
P.O. Box 3837
Modesto, CA 95352

Prentice Hall Allyn & Bacon
Equipment Division
10 Oriskany Drive
Tonawanda, NY 14150-6781

Schoolmasters Science
P.O. Box 1941
Ann Arbor, MI 48106

Science Kit & Boreal Laboratories
777 East Park Drive
Tonawanda, NY 14150-6782 or
P.O. Box 2726
Santa Fe Springs, CA 90670-4490

Wards Natural Science Establishment, Inc.
5100 West Henrietta Road
P.O. Box 92912
Rochester, NY 14692

Bibliography

Ardley, Neil. *Exploring Magnetism.* New York: Watts, 1983.

Asimov, Isaac. *How Did We Find Out About Electricity?* New York: Walker, 1973

Beller, Joel. *So You Want to Do a Science Project.* New York: Arco, 1982.

Bombaugh, Ruth. *Science Fair Success.* Hillside, N.J.: Enslow, 1990

Catherall, Ed. *Magnets.* Morristown, N.J.: Silver Burdett, 1982.

Herbert, Don. *Mr. Wizard's Supermarket Science.* New York: Random House, 1980.

Hogan, Paula Z. *Inventions that Changed Our Lives: The Compass.* New York: Walker, 1982.

Laron, Carl. *Electronics Basics.* Englewood Cliffs, N.J.: Prentice-Hall, 1984.

Leon, Goerge deLucenay. *The Electricity Story: 2500 Years of Experiments and Discoveries.* New York: Arco, 1983.

Math, Irwin. *More Wires and Watts: Understanding and Using Electricity.* New York: Scribner's, 1988.

Reuben, Gabriel. *Electricity Experiments for Children.* New York: Dover, 1968.

Tocci, Salvatore. *How to Do a Science Fair Project.* New York: Watts, 1986.

Van Deman, B.A., and E. McDonald. *Nuts and Bolts: A Matter of Fact Guide to Science Fair Projects.* Harwood Heights, IL: Science Man Press, 1980.

Webster, David. *How to Do a Science Project.* New York: Watts, 1974.

Index

About the Author

Robert Gardner is a retired high school teacher of physics, chemistry and physical science. He has taught in a number of National Science Foundation teachers' institutes and is an award-winning author of science books for young people.